Shipping Container Homes

A Simple Guide to Build a Customized, Eco-Friendly, Sustainable, and Affordable House. Avoid Daily Stress and Live in Your Dream Home with Your Family

Written by:

Theo Skeldon

Introduction 10

Chapter 1.   Why Choose Shipping Container Homes 15

   Accessibility 15

   Incredible Space 16

   Time-Saving 16

   Affordable to Build 17

   Friendly for the Setting (Green Living) 17

   Weather-Proof 17

   Excellent Flexibility 19

Chapter 2.   How to Start the Project 20

   Go See an Actual Shipping Container 20

   Review Building Regulations and Construction Codes That Apply to the Prospective Building Site 21

   Determine the Budget 21

   Do a Physical Survey of the Building Site 22

   Decide on the Exact Project Requirements 23

   Create a Layout and Floor Plan 23

   Finalize the Design 23

Chapter 3.   Site Preparation 25

   Deciding the Location 26

   Shade and Sun 26

Site Work 26

Staking and Marking 27

Grubbing and Clearing 27

Grading, Cutting, and Filling 27

Soil Types 28

Gravel 28

Rock 28

Sandy Soil 29

Clay 29

Septic and Sewer 29

Chapter 4. Pay Attention! 30

Questions to Ask Yourself 30

What Are Your Needs? 30

Where Will the Home Be Built? 30

What's Your Budget? 31

When Would You Like to Have Your Home Completed? 31

Can You Pull It Off? 31

Financial Planning 31

Permits and Zoning Laws 33

Australia 33

New Zealand 33

3

United Kingdom	34
United States	34
General List of Documents Required	34
Designing Your Home	35

Chapter 5. Sample Plans 37

Plan 1	37
Plan 2	39
Plan 3	40
Plan 4	42
Plan 5	44
Plan 6	46
Plan 7	48
Plan 8	50
Plan 9	52
Plan 10	55
Plan 11	57
Plan 12	59
Plan 13	61
Plan 14	63
Plan 15	64
Plan 16	66

Plan 17 68

Plan 18 70

Plan 19 71

Plan 20 73

Chapter 6.   Foundation 75

Concrete Piers 75

Slab-on-Grade 76

Pile Foundation 77

Strip Foundation 77

Concrete Foundation 78

Footings 79

Fixing the Container 82

Chapter 7.   Receiving Container 83

Prefab Containers 83

On-Site Conversion 84

Off-Site Conversion 85

Shipping 87

Buy Local 87

Cost 88

Plan Ahead 88

Container Placement 89

Tilting 89

Cranes 89

Anchoring the Containers 91

Welding 91

Bolting 92

Clamping 93

Chapter 8.   Insulation 94

What Does Insulation Actually Achieve: Understanding R-Value 94

Batting Insulation 95

Foam Insulation 95

Natural Insulation Methods 97

Cotton and Wool Insulation 97

Straw Bale Insulation 98

Insulation Panels 99

Chapter 9.   Services: Electricity, Plumbing, and Phone Line 100

First Fix Services 100

Installing First Fix Services 103

Electric and Telephone Services 103

Installing Your Drains 105

Water Line Installation 107

Telephone Line Services 108

Second Fix Services 109

Electric Services 110

Plumbing 112

Chapter 10.   Renewable Energies 114

Solar Panels: Hot Water and Electricity 114

How Much Solar Power Do I Need? 116

Installing Solar Panels 116

Assemble Your System Before You Install It 117

Chapter 11.   Flooring 119

Replacing the Plywood Floors 119

Keeping the Plywood Floor 120

Install Subfloors 121

Treating the Original Floors 122

Concrete 122

Finishing Touches 123

Adding Tiles 124

Carpeting 126

Laminate Floors 127

Chapter 12.   Rooftop 129

Pros 129

Cons 130

Roof Types 130

Preparing for a "Green" Roof 131

Flat Roofing 132

Sloped or Shed/Angled Roofing 132

Chapter 13.   Interiors 134

Adjoining Containers 134

Installation of an Auxiliary Container Joining Structure 135

Floors 136

Doors and Windows 137

Making the Openings 138

How to Make the Frames 139

How to Install Doors and Windows 139

Chapter 14.   Exterior 140

Finishing an Exterior with External Insulation 140

Painting Exterior Insulation 140

Rendering or Stuccoing the Exterior 141

Finishing an Exterior without External Insulation 142

Painting Your Container 143

Timber Cladding Your Exterior 143

Chapter 15.   Tips in Choosing a Container 145

Price of Containers 146

Size of the Container 146

Type of the Container 147

Condition of the Container 148

Chapter 16.   Organization and Design Hacks for Your Container Home 149

Bedroom 149

Living Area 151

Kitchen 152

Bathroom 155

Conclusion **158**

Introduction

In this busy world, we live in today the land that is available for real estate is quickly diminishing as the population keeps increasing across the globe. Overpopulation is causing living conditions to become difficult for many and overcrowding is becoming more of a concern with each passing day. The more people we have in our world the fewer places we are going to have available to live in. The prices of houses are sky rocketing to the point that many cannot afford to buy them or even rent them. Many people are living on the streets of major cities because they are unable to afford rent.

If you are seriously interested in building your own container home then why not do it right from the start? I hope to accomplish helping you do this through the information in this book. Let us now move into the world of containers and get to know what they are really all about so you will be able to make a shipping container home that you will be proud of!

It is always a good idea to do some research first before you run into a project with blinders on. To make sure that you are not going to make bad choices that could end up being disastrous for you I have some tips and suggestions within these pages that I hope will offer you secure guidelines that you can follow when making decisions regarding the building of your shipping container home. To avoid bad situations while working on a project it will certainly be worth your while to read this book. You have certainly taken a step in the right direction to help ensure that you are off to a good start with the building of your shipping container home just by downloading this book.

Many people may jump into living in a container home with the expectation that it is going to solve all of their housing problems. This in fact is just not true. Like many other human dwellings container homes come with their benefits as well as issues. If you have the expectation that it will all, be wonderful and perfect then you may be setting yourself up for disappointment. You need to go into this with an open mind and be realistic in knowing that there will be issues with living in a container home. You need to decide if these are issues that you can live with or not.

You do not want to find yourself rushing in to buy a container home only to find out that it is not the home that you expected it to be. However, people that have more realistic views are happy living in their metal box homes. In the end, of course, whether you are happy in your container home will be up to you. You need to decide if this kind of home will suit your needs. Since this is going to be a life-changing decision I suggest that you take time to really mull things over to make a clearer decision.

Asking questions is going to help you make a clearer decision on whether living in a container home is the right choice in living accommodation for you. You need to really know if you can truly commit fully to this kind of lifestyle. It is best to go into it with eyes wide open. Once you have completed your research it is time to get down to making this project of building your own container home come to life.

You need to look at your financial situation and decide whether you can afford to build your container home. Are you going to be able to do all or most of the work involved yourself? Are you going to have to hire professionals to work on it? Where are you looking to locate it? Once you have made your decision to live in a container home there are going to be many questions that you will have to ask yourself along the way. Ask local government officials to find out what it would cost to build your container home in the area you want to build it.

When it comes to turning a shipping container into your home it is going to certainly come with its advantages and disadvantages. Most information regarding containers tends to lean one way or the other in terms of the pros and cons of living in a container home. Some will say there are no issues with living in a container home. Others will have a list of problems that they have associated with living in a container home.

We will view it objectively so that you are able to understand exactly what you are getting into. Your optimism will be raised I am sure when you see the advantages that will be listed here. On the other hand, the disadvantages listed may make you think twice about making the commitment to live in a container home. You may even decide to abandon the idea altogether. The aim of this list is to offer you a realistic view of what you should be prepared to expect when you create a home out of metal boxes.

Advantages of living in a container home:

- The cost for you to create a container home is much lower than what it would cost you to build a conventional home that has roughly the same square footage and materials to use.
- The dimensions of the containers are pretty uniform so you should be able to stack them up without any problems.
- The materials are easy to transport from one area to another.

Disadvantages of living in a container home:

- The size of the containers is uncompromising.
- You will not have a lot of flexibility with container size, so you will need to get containers that will work with your plan.
- Containers are expensive.
- It can be tough working with containers, cutting through a lot of metal. You will need to add bracings to strengthen the structure.
- There is no insulation.
- You may need to get containers cleaned to make sure that they are rid of any hazardous materials left over time.
- They are not very attractive looking in their basic form.

Chapter 1.   Why Choose Shipping Container Homes

Living in a home constructed with recycled shipping containers has plenty of advantages, and more people are beginning to understand this and take action. You will appreciate these advantages first-hand and see them for yourself if you are lucky enough to have created your own and/or live in one.

It is now possible to use shipping containers for other purposes. These containers are now one of the best choices, considering the limited space and growing costs of building houses or offices. There were rumors that a branch of Starbucks was only made up of 2 containers. Looking at the interior design of the container, it looked like an elegant place to rest.

This makes them ideal for architectural homes as well. They deliver minimal costs for building material, plus can be easily changed. With 2 containers, you'll already have a nice location. While there were formerly prefabricated buildings, they were never intended as a place to conduct business.

I'll outline some of the advantages of living in used shipping containers:

Accessibility

The best price tag for building materials vs. steel containers will be the latter. You face financial difficulties each time you build a house; this will minimize the house's cost in so many ways.

Incredible Space

As it is rectangular, the room can be created easily. Instead of making it from scratch, the container can send you various sizes, forming unique forms for your property. You can get the 20 x 40 containers in your main room and get other sizes for your other rooms. Since these things can be bundled together, you can maximize the efficiency of your space.

Time-Saving

It takes time to construct a traditional building. From the moment the base is built to the end of the concrete supporting beams, there is no house or office. Prefabricated structures such as containers can easily become functional offices if you quickly need office space. This saves lag in the house-building process. The building of a metal container can quickly become an elegant room.

The average time to prepare and transport a shipping container is in the range of 2 months. This involves the time from the initial purchase to the complete personalization to create a comfortable home or office environment.

Furthermore, many companies are specializing in fitting containers for the fastest performance. It is nevertheless possible for those who want a more hands-on approach to fully complete the fit when the container is shipped and located.

Affordable to Build

The average cost of this sort of home or office is very affordable. It is cheaper to purchase a container and turn it into a secure and comfortable home than to buy a normal property in a cheap town area.

Used container homes are more economical to produce than traditional methods of construction.

Friendly for the Setting (Green Living)

So how green can vibrant shipping containers be?

Response: They can be as green as you would like them to be.

Think of your home more like an "eco-pod" if you want to go down a very green path. By placing a few solar panels on the roof, you could generate your electricity. If you're close to a river or a quick-flowing stream, you can use hydro.

A 'Green/Living Roof' can be added to the top of your containers to help separate and drastically reduce heating and cooling costs in the winter (in the summer).

Weather-Proof

Consider the fact that shipping containers on hundreds of thousands of miles of open-top trans-oceanic shipping container vessels are designed to endure the most unforgiving environmental conditions and constructed before being decommissioned to have a minimum work life of 20 years. After that, these containers have an almost endless lifespan, in a fixed location.

They are made from prefabricated steel and welded, making them strong and rigid, and very durable. This makes them especially well-suited for high geologic activity areas, such as hurricane hotspots and earthquake zones.

Shipping containers can keep up to 175 mph (281 km/h) safely against wind speeds when anchored to pylons, which is easy to do. Whether it is constructed from used shipping containers or a conventional building, each building should have adequate foundations.

I listed the three main advantages above that most homeowners would note immediately. In truth, they are the three key things many people look at when buying any kind of home. It also reveals that the boom in shipping container homes has been entirely justifiable in the last few years and why so many individuals turn to these containers to create their own dream homes.

With the right internal floor plans, a comfortable and practical space can be created, with everything you need to relax in style.

Although it can sound like there are many difficulties in turning a container into a home, the whole process is usually straightforward. Once the secondary container has been purchased and shipped to your territory, it is simply a process of acquiring the correct plans for the intended purpose. The professionals will benefit from a high-quality finish. Moreover, experts would certainly need to install windows, doors, power supplies, and the like.

Excellent Flexibility

If the container has been purchased, the internal configuration and most essential features can be customized. It typically helps to look at various floor plans and floor sizes to understand what is available and create the layout to meet your particular needs. The traditional 20 ft. container is an excellent way to turn it into a house since it is simpler to navigate and is better suited for combining it with other units.

The 40 ft. model is a choice for those looking for more interior space and provides access to almost 300 square ft. of space. Also, the wider container provides more versatility in separating internal space into different spaces.

Chapter 2.   How to Start the Project

Planning is the real key to a build that is efficient, economical, and achievable. Even before coming up with a design plan, there are many factors that need to be considered. Proper preparation ensures that the build goes smoothly when it is actually underway.

In the Pre-Design stage, the goal is to come up with the concept for the design. The input of those involved in the actual construction—including designers, contractors, and equipment or material suppliers—is taken into account, along with the expectations of the future homeowners and the money they are willing to spend.

All in all, this will result in a complete profile of the project: the scope, the budget, and the risks and difficulties to be potentially experienced during the build.

That said, figuring out where to begin can be daunting, especially for a first construction project. Following this checklist can be a great way to get started.

Go See an Actual Shipping Container

Obviously, shipping containers are needed to build a shipping container home. That is why the first step is to find an actual container and give it a thorough examination. Get a concrete idea of what the space really looks like. This will help in figuring out the overall design later and in keeping expectations in the realm of the feasible.

This is also a chance to compare the quality and price of containers from different sources, should there be more than one in an area. When surveying used containers, keep an eye out for ones that have minimal damage. These may cost a little more, but it is better than going cheap and then overspending on repairs.

Review Building Regulations and Construction Codes That Apply to the Prospective Building Site

A lot will depend on the location of the build. Contact the local building or planning department and inquire about mandatory permits and inspections, as well as any building restrictions. Mention that the home to be constructed has modular steel components and ask if this will lead to any pre-construction issues.

As a rule, most governing bodies grant landowners the right to build almost any type of residence on privately owned property. However, in some cases, a Certificate of Occupancy may be required. To obtain it, it is necessary to follow building and zoning regulations.

Height limitations, maximum square footage, even the number of bathrooms allowed, are all examples of the kind of information that is vital in coming up with a final design.

Determine the Budget

It's easy to just name a price and call it the budget, but really, that's not how things should be done.

Coming up with a budget requires a look at every aspect of the build. Get an idea of the construction, labor, and professional fees. Take note of everything that needs to be done, what materials will be required and exactly how many people will be needed. Minimize the risk of incurring unexpected expenses by being as thorough as possible.

Consulting architects and contractors is a great way to get a more concrete idea of how much a project will cost. It is also advisable to get in contact with companies who sell containers and do modifications.

It is best to keep the budget a little below the amount of money that is actually available. This margin will cover any unanticipated expenses that are to be expected during any construction project.

Do a Physical Survey of the Building Site

The choice of a building site is crucial. One big factor to consider is the soil bearing capacity—referring to the capacity of the soil to support the structural load applied to the ground.

Other features of the site, such as the landscape and greenery, can be taken advantage of to provide not only an aesthetic appeal but a practical one as well. For example, clumps of trees can naturally provide shade and decrease winter chill when taken into account in the design.

The location of a house will also determine the ease of access and the degree of privacy. Try to see how far the site is from the road or highway. Will it be necessary to add an extended driveway? Concerns like this can increase the cost of the build and should be taken into account during budgeting.

Decide on the Exact Project Requirements

Get started on a 'wish list'. In particular, focus on the number of rooms that are needed. Decide on how many bedrooms and bathrooms there will be, and on whether rooms will be constructed for utilities like the kitchen and dining area. Detail any additional features desired, such as a home office space, a game room, or the like. Estimate the rough square footage required for each, and for the whole project.

However, prepare to negotiate. Most likely, adjustments will need to be made in coming up with the final design or during the build. Try your best to be flexible and to be open to new ideas and suggestions from professionals.

Create a Layout and Floor Plan

Once the 'wish list' is ready, start sketching a layout and floor plan for the home. Make sure to draw the dimensions to scale. This will give a better idea of what the finished product will actually look like after completion.

Remember to incorporate all the functional elements that should be in the home, outlining the correct number of rooms and their purpose. Incorporate as many ideas as possible, but don't overcrowd the space. The key to a comfortable living area is a balanced utilization of space. Even a room with a small area can feel relatively expansive with a successful interior layout.

Finalize the Design

A general idea is all well and good, but once that's done, it's time to get into the specifics.

One is to hire an architect to come up with the design based on the outlined specifications. This has the advantage of producing a completely unique and original home that will cater to specific needs or preferences.

However, there is a downside. Since shipping container homes are still relatively rare, it may be a challenge to find someone who is willing and able to design the home. There are many design considerations unique to shipping container homes that the average architect—no matter how skilled—may be unfamiliar with.

An alternative is to locate a design entity that offers turnkey home designs. 'Turnkey' means the design is ready to use once purchased. The source company will offer several 'stock' designs to choose from. These ready-made 'kit' designs can then be adapted to the building site.

Although this doesn't allow for extensive customization, it has the advantage of taking less time and costing less overall. Should there be non-negotiable aspects of the home, which should absolutely be included in the design, look for a company that is willing to customize, although this will probably increase the cost.

Additionally, having the final design is essential in coming up with the final budget. These plans and drawings, among other documents, are also needed in applying for building permits and getting authorization for construction.

Chapter 3.   Site Preparation

There is a great amount of site work that needs to be done before you can start working on your shipping container home. If you fail to think about and execute all these in the early stages of the project, you might have to deal with some costly rework at a later stage. At the topmost level, the preparation and site planning you opt for at this stage is mainly intended to make sure that the land is completely prepared for the building site. You will need to opt for site preparation so that the land is ready for the containers. There are several factors that you need to consider while preparing the site for your container home.

Deciding the Location

Before you can make your mind to start working on the actual home, you will have to determine where you want to place your shipping containers.

Shade and Sun

Depending on the climate, the sun might turn out to be both a curse and a blessing. It might end up warming you up on a cool morning. However, it might also blind you while having your morning beverage. It can deliver natural and soft lighting in the interior spaces; however, it might also result in a solar thermal gain that will cost you extra air conditioning. As you begin narrowing down the probable building sites on the property, try to figure out the way in which the sun interacts with every area at various times of the day. Shades from nearby bushes and trees can make some huge differences. Keep in mind that the shade will get reduced when deciduous trees start shedding their leaves during winter and fall.

Site Work

Under the site work, you will be considering all sorts of physical work that you will need to get done with the building site along with the surrounding areas. Relying on the dirt type that needs to be removed, the utilities need to be installed, and the direction of approach, it will make more sense to do one thing at a time.

Staking and Marking

The first step is to mark all the corners where you will be placing your shipping containers. You will also have to mark the locations of the existing and planned utilities, other buildings, roads, etc. For a part of this, you might have to get in touch with some utility locating companies that can assist you to know where you have the gas pipelines, water mains, or some other buried utilities. Such utilities are not affiliated with the project; however, they just pass through your property. You can use ground marking paints for a better idea, along with wooden stakes. You can join them with strings to get a better picture of the larger areas. After you are done with marking the building site, you will know where you have to work for the next steps.

Grubbing and Clearing

In this step, you will have to clear all sorts of debris, vegetation, and obstacles from the marked areas. It will involve the removal of bushes, trees, rocks, junk, and other things that might get in your way. It can be done easily by getting a contractor. However, if you want to save money, you can do it yourself. The more is the vegetation in your area, the more you will have to work. You will also have to think about what to do with all the things that you collect. You can cut the vegetation into small pieces and use them for compost. The big pieces can be used as firewood. You can also pile up everything and bury them, burn them, or haul them away.

Grading, Cutting, and Filling

After you are done with clearing out everything that comes in your way of the building site, you can start seeing what you need to work with. Relying on the type of foundation that you have opted for, a building site that is uneven in nature might turn out to be a problem for you. But if you are opting for slab foundation or something of that sort, you will have to do some grading work and develop a properly leveled building pad. In this stage, you will also have to think about your drainage planning. To control the water flow, you might have to add berms and swales to protect the shipping containers and redirect water from the same. Also, you will have to start working on the access road. You will need to pick a route that is right for you.

You might have to install bridges, culverts, or low-water crossings if there is any place where water flows.

Soil Types

The soil of your building site might be filled with clay or sandy. Also, it might be filled up with rocks or even solid rocks. What you need to know is that each of the soil types can handle weight in different ways. So, it is extremely important to know what the soil type of your location can actually handle before starting on the plans.

Gravel

It is a coarse-grained material that can provide you with superb drainage. It is quite easy to dig out to your required depth and also level it for the foundation of your home.

Rock

Working with a rocky surface might turn out to be a bit challenging. However, it will be a blessing for you if the building site is a slab of rock. All you need to do is to strip any soil surface, level the pad, and you are ready to go. Rock comes with some great load-bearing capacity. It can also support any kind of foundation. If your contractor still recommends you to use supports, you can opt for concrete piers.

Sandy Soil

It is composed of fine-grained particles, often with some rock and gravel mixed in. It can support a huge amount of weight only if the weight is distributed over a large area.

Clay

It is very fine-grained and can hold a lot of water. Your contractor might ask you to dig down the clay part and then backfill with other suitable soil. You can opt for a concrete pile foundation for clay soil.

Septic and Sewer

If your home location offers access to some nearby sewer lines, you will have to determine the cost along with the process of tying in. For rural areas, a septic system might be your only available option. The majority of septic systems include a buried tank or several tanks along with a buried line with sprinklers or leach pipes. Consult with your contractor to find a good location for your septic system.

You will have to pay proper attention to the site preparation as it will form the base of your entire shipping container home. Even the smallest mistakes might cost you a huge sum afterward.

Chapter 4.   Pay Attention!

In order to know how you'd like to build your shipping container home; the first step is to plan it out. This means asking a few questions, exploring some of the practical needs and considerations before entering into the design phase.

Questions to Ask Yourself

To get you started with this, here are some of the most important things to take into consideration:

What Are Your Needs?

Consider how many bedrooms you want, how much floor space you and your family will require.

Consider the number of bathrooms and the extent of storage space necessary.

With a shipping container home, space is at a premium, so you'll want to consider how you can accommodate all of your needs as efficiently as possible.

Where Will the Home Be Built?

This question influences a number of other considerations, including zoning requirements for your intended location, soil type and foundation, and utility planning.

What's Your Budget?

This is another key consideration, as it will determine how many containers you can use, whether or not you will be able to hire contractors to help with the work, whether you intend to buy new, used, or one-time use containers, and a number of other factors.

When Would You Like to Have Your Home Completed?

Timing is crucial when considering container delivery, equipment rental, and contracting arrangements.

Remember that in most instances, shipping container homes can be built in a matter of days or at most weeks.

Can You Pull It Off?

Do you have access to the skills, materials, financial resources, planning permission, and other necessities required for construction?

Financial Planning

What can you afford? In most instances, this will determine your budget. Key considerations will include the cost of the land, the container, and the roof. Other important considerations are whether you have the skills, time, and resources to do the modification yourself, if you would like to hire contractors for the work, or if you intend to purchase the container pre-modified as a home.

The following highlights a number of design choices and other factors which have a decisive impact upon the budget. Among these factors are whether you choose to purchase a new, used, or one-time-use container, whether to include a roof and the degree of modification you would like done to the container.

Here is the budget used for the real-life example depicted above. This will give you a better idea of some of the possible costs.

Component	Quantity	Expenditure
Land (including taxes and fees)	1	$8000
Fees to professionals		$6500
Standard 40 Foot Container (Used in US)	2	$6300
Bathroom		$2500
Door (for both inside and outside)	5	$700
Kitchen		$3000
Insulation	1	$1800
Furniture		$3800
Windows	4	$850
Utilities		$3500
Internal fixes and fittings		$1500
Transport		$500
Flooring		$2300
Roof		$5500
Paint		$700
Walls inside home		$300
Unexpected costs	12%	$5730
Summary		$53480

One thing to remember regarding the example above is that the furnishings, flooring, and interior design have been chosen with luxury rather than the economy in mind. Note that a 10% contingency cost has been added. Most construction endeavors, regardless of how well planned, include some unexpected expenses, so it's helpful to make sure you're prepared for such things when they occur.

Permits and Zoning Laws

Each country and, in most cases, each zoning district within a country has its own zoning regulations. These regulations determine which types of buildings can be placed on a given lot, as well as the density, height, and other requirements for structures within the zone. These regulations are complex, and it is not possible to provide all the details for every zone. However, here are a few details that will give some direction in becoming knowledgeable about your country's guidelines. Also included is a list of documents that are likely to be required by any country when designing your home.

Australia

Prior to major building work in Australia, you must obtain a permit from the local council. Check into your state's policy planning framework online, and then approach the council to find out the requirements for your state and for the council which governs your intended building site. They will be able to provide you with a list of any documents required for your area or any regulations which should be considered during the design and planning phases.

New Zealand

New Zealand is a bit ahead of the game when it comes to shipping container homes. The Building Act of 2004 offers clear guidance for the construction of these homes. In most cases, they will require building consent, though if they are intended only for storage, then they may be exempt from this requirement. In addition, the territorial authority may choose to exempt your shipping container home from building consent, so long as it still meets the building codes. As in the examples above, the first step is to confer with the territorial authority to look into the specifics of your intended site and design.

United Kingdom

Any construction in the UK will require permission from the local council. The local planning authorities will each have their own specific regulations, so it is necessary to contact them before design and planning. The list of documents provided below will give you a head start, and they will be able to inform you if anything further is required.

United States

For most places in the U.S., construction requires a building permit. In order to obtain a building permit, first, contact the local public works department.

If your building site is outside the city's zoning code, then it may not require a building permit. If you seek to build without a permit, then deliberately selecting a site outside of the zoning code is one way to avoid a bit of red tape.

General List of Documents Required

Though each council or local authority will have its own specifications and regulations, here are a few things you can expect to need. Remember that regulations may influence aspects of design, so it still helps to approach your local authority before spending valuable time and energy finalizing your design.

- Structural engineering plans and approval
- Site plan
- Building regulation drawings (to scale)
- Before and after elevations
- Fully dimensioned working drawings

Designing Your Home

So, once you've considered your needs and done your homework with regard to the local regulations, it's time to begin designing your home. Here is where you can get really creative. The simplest design would be a single container home, and the sky's the limit on how far you can go with it. Two-story? Three? The possibilities are endless and they can be customized to fit your needs, whatever they might be.

It's most common to stick with single-story homes and to place containers next to one another until you reach your desired size. Connecting walls can be removed to increase the floor space of a room, and interior walls can be added to partition a container into multiple rooms. The basics are the bedroom, living room, kitchen, bathroom, and pantry, and all of these can be fit within a single 20 ft container if you're comfortable with a cozy living space.

A quick search online will offer many free software downloads that will help you to design your shipping container home. If you're uncomfortable doing this yourself, then you may want to factor the price of an architect into the budget. Usually, the quotes for such a small living space won't be unreasonable. However, give it a try and see how it works for you. You may be surprised how easy it is to design your home, and being in the driver's seat of the design process can be really fun.

Here are a number of sample plans which offer a wide range of different designs:

Chapter 5.   Sample Plans

It takes a little bit of clever maneuvering to fit everything a home needs inside a single shipping container. But it can be done, and quite nicely, without sacrificing anything important. For some, the idea of working it all out themselves is a big part of the draw. Perhaps while reading this book, you have been designing your own house inside your head. But if you are having a hard time visualizing how it will look when it all comes together, there are ways you can study. Not that any of these need to be followed to the letter, but they are certainly good for gathering ideas. Below are some sample floor plans you can have a look at

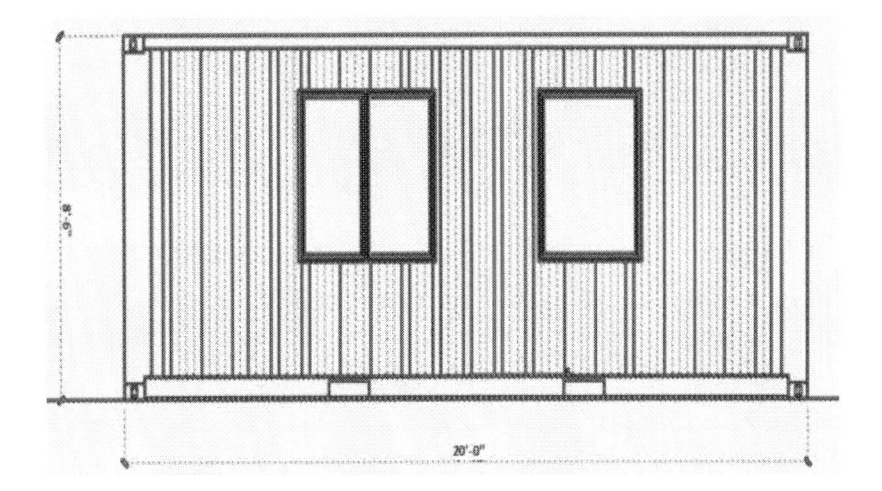

Plan 1

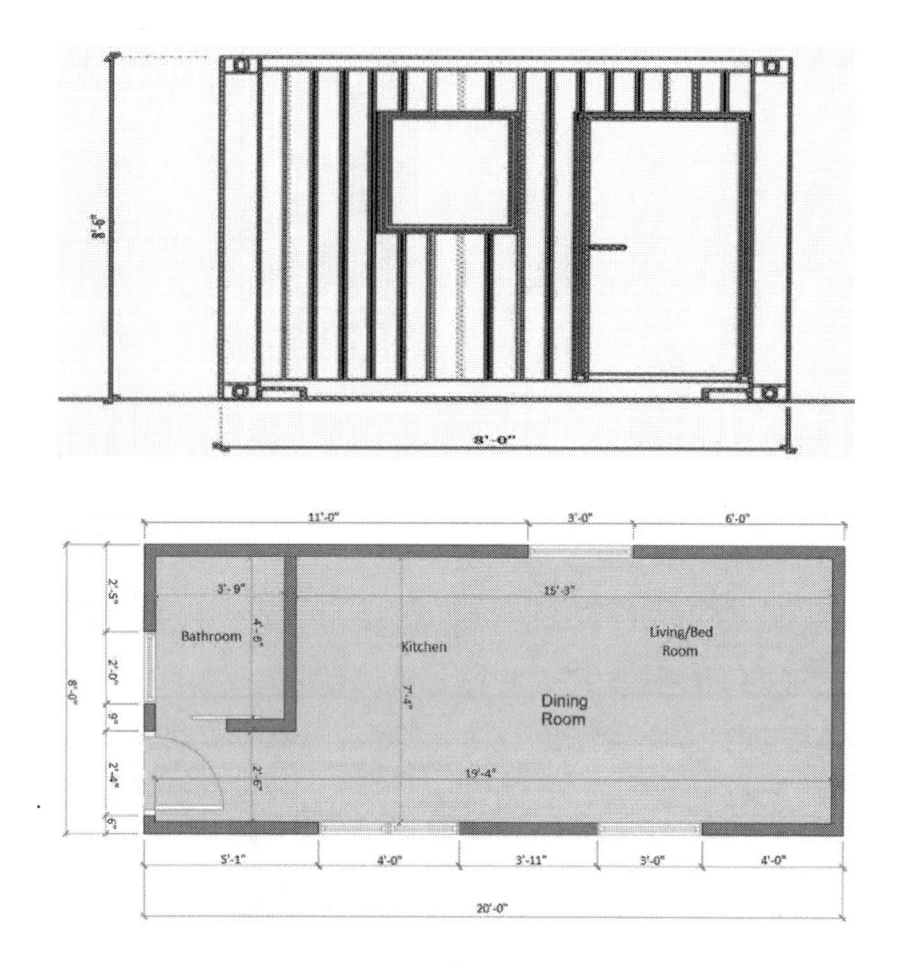

Plan 1 is ideal for a small, one-person dwelling. It offers 139 sq. ft. and is designed from a single 20 ft container and features a combination kitchen, dining room, living room, and bedroom. The ultimate in space efficiency and tiny living space.

Plan 2

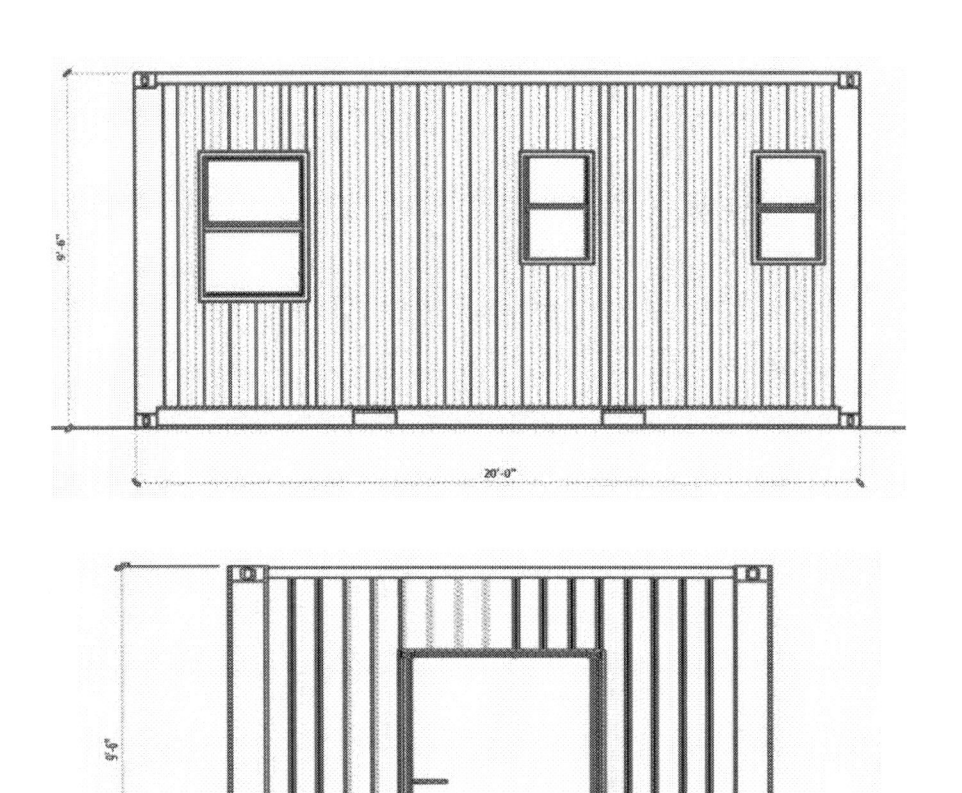

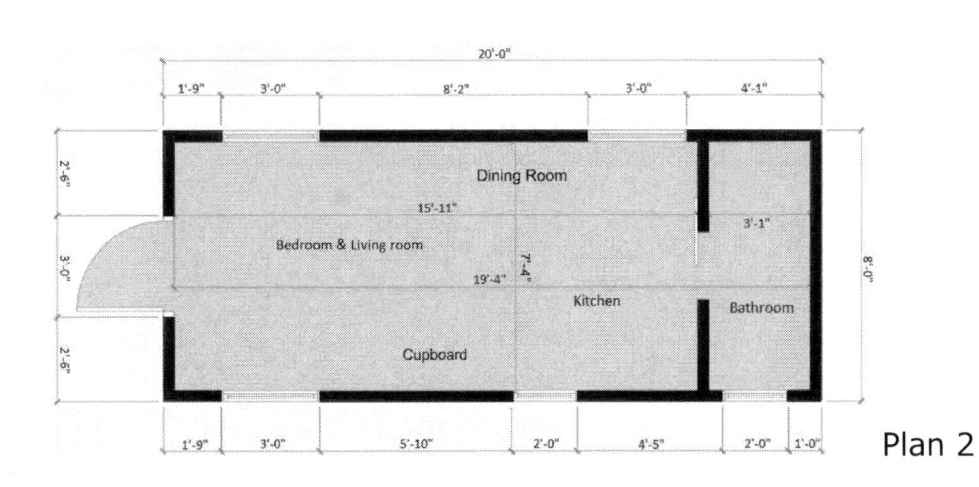

Plan 2

This is another example of a single 20 ft container dwelling. It has been customized to offer a spacious bathroom and kitchen. The living room doubles as a bedroom and features 2 pull-out double beds, offering comfort whether sleeping or sitting. This economical design can comfortably house 2 people within 138 sq. ft.

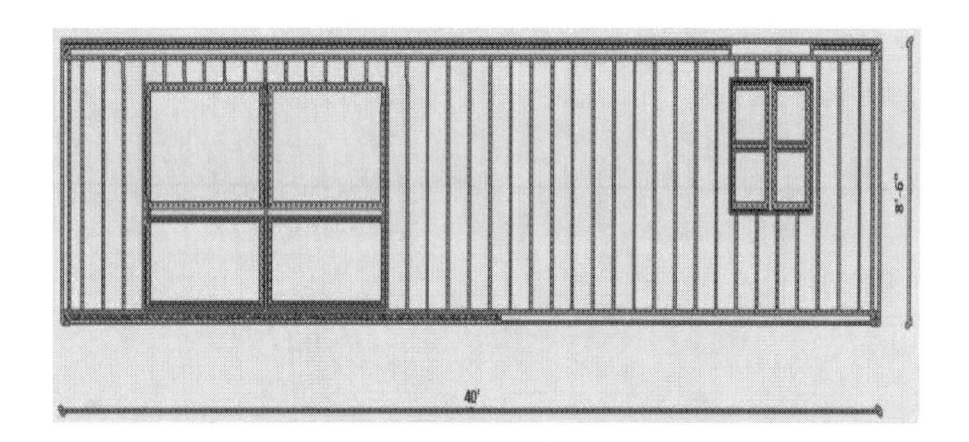

Plan 3

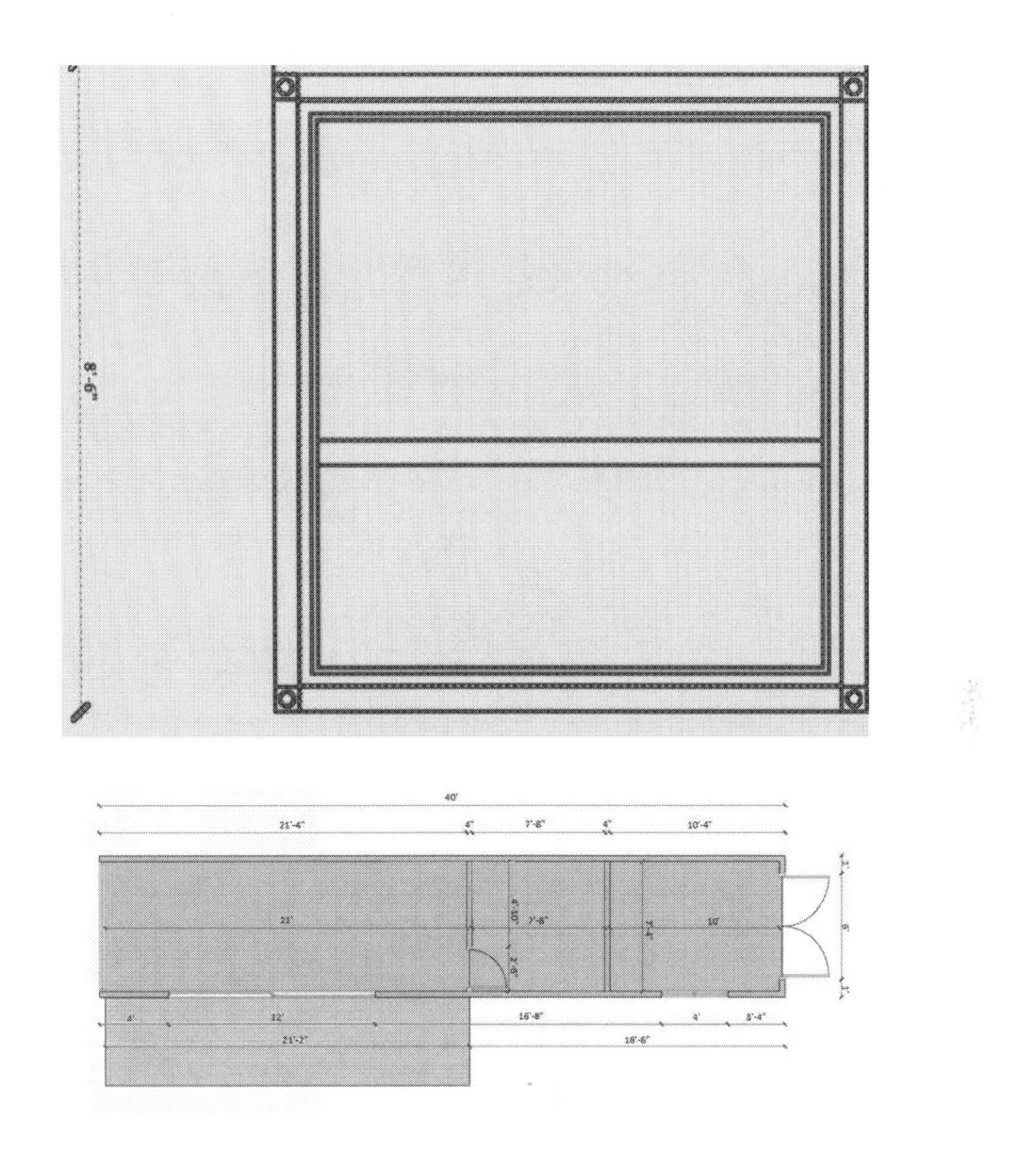

Plan 3 is designed from a single 40 ft. container and boasts a spacious open-plan living room which would be ideal for a sofa bed. It features sliding glass doors which lead to an open deck. Also included is a second room ideal either for storage space or for a second bedroom.

Plan 4

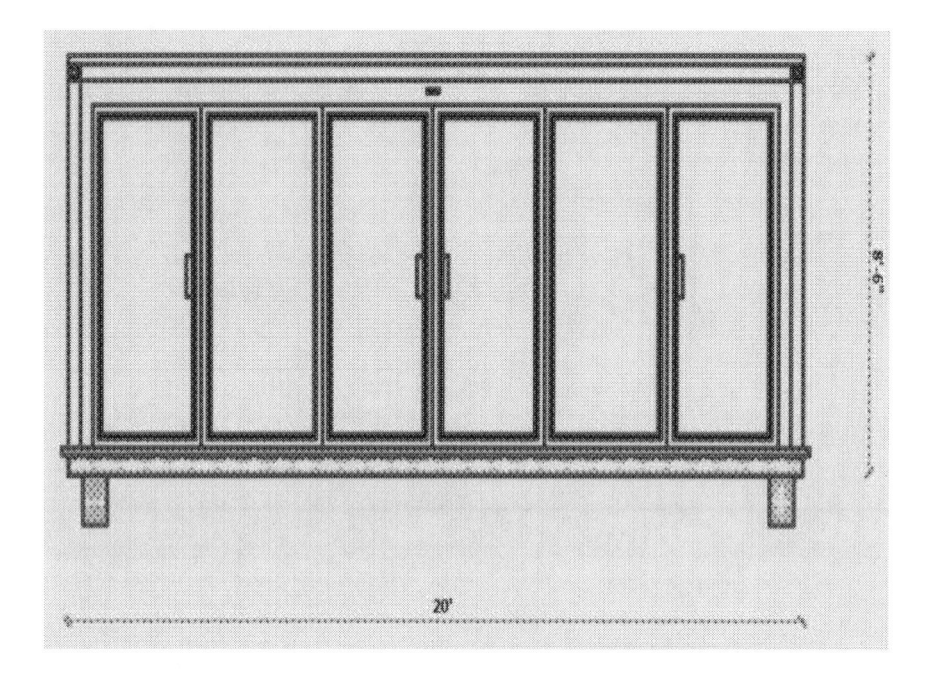

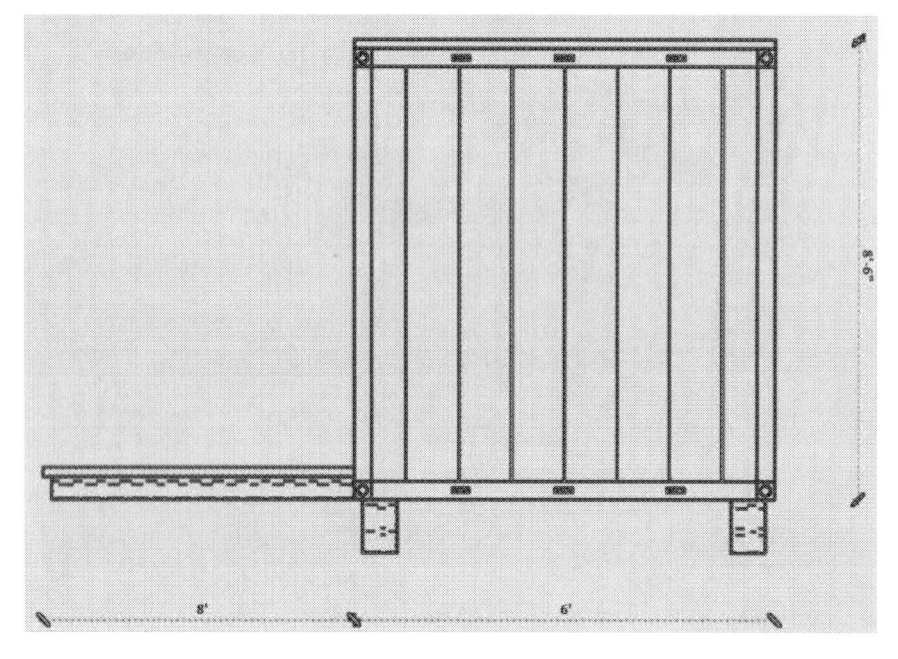

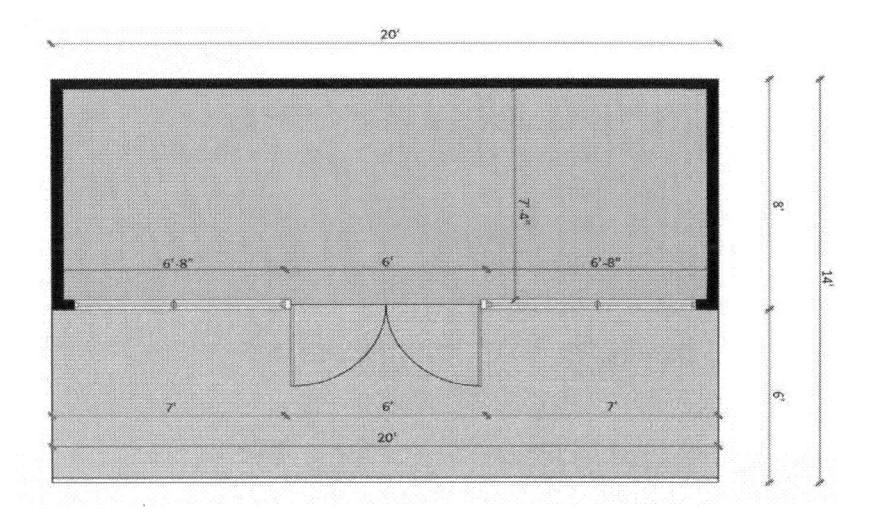

Plan 4 has been designed as a hunting lodge from a single 20 ft. container. It features a large open-plan living room with a small kitchen and bedroom off to the side. A full-length deck lines the front of the house, making it ideal for relaxing comfortably and taking in the night air. This offers a luxurious space for a single-person dwelling and can offer a comfortable space for 2 if a sofa bed is placed in the living room.

Plan 5

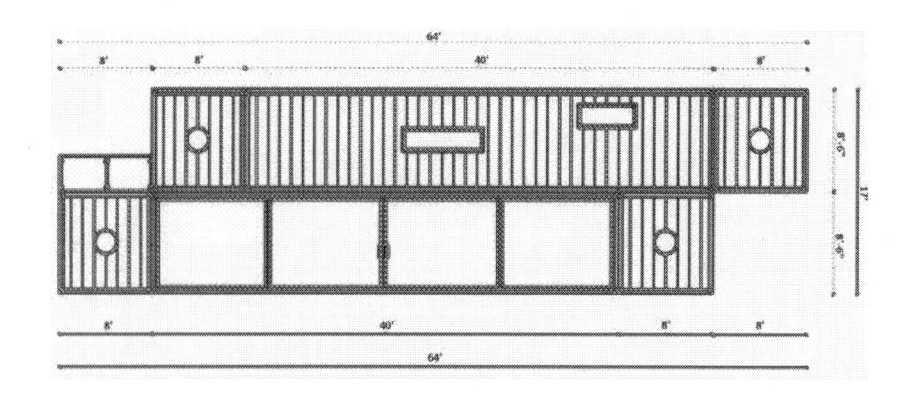

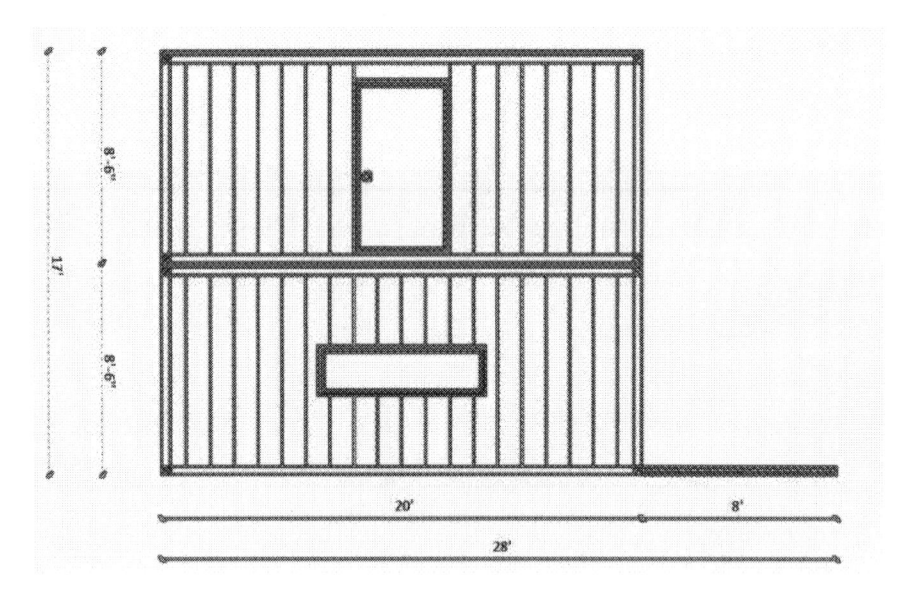

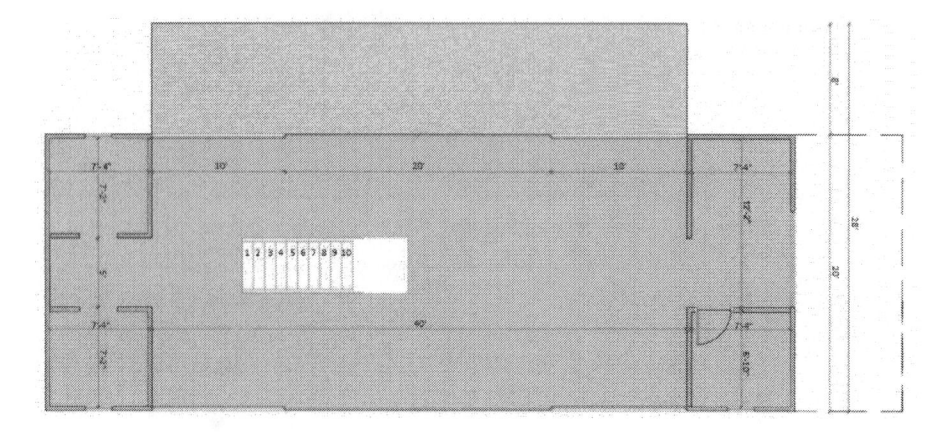

44

Upstairs:

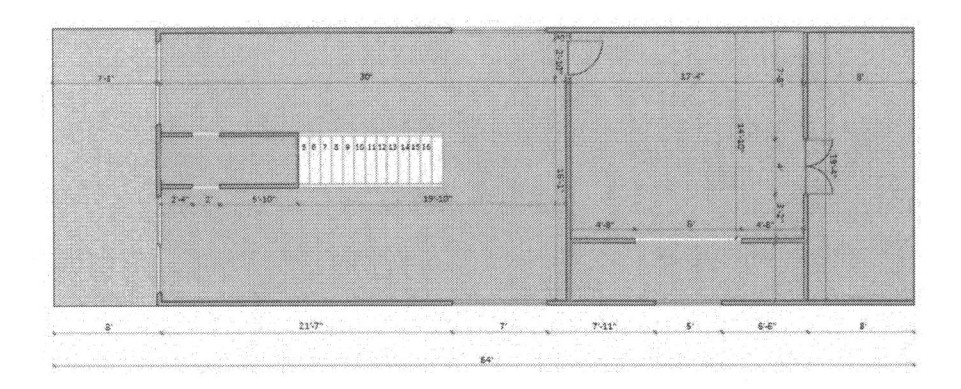

Plan 5 has been designed from 4 40 ft. containers and 4 20 ft. containers. It demonstrates the luxury possible with shipping container homes. This mansion features 2 floors, 3 bedrooms, 3 bathrooms, and an open-plan living room on both floors. Sliding glass doors on both the front and rear entrance and a second-floor deck make this design equal to any traditional home built with the height of decadence.

Plan 6

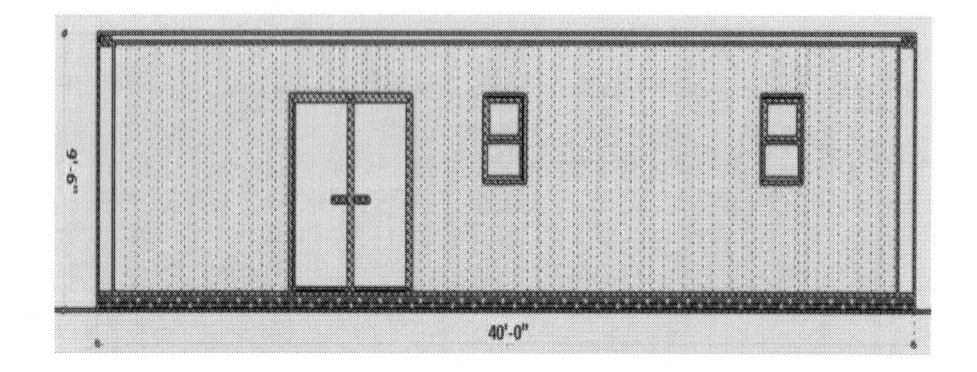

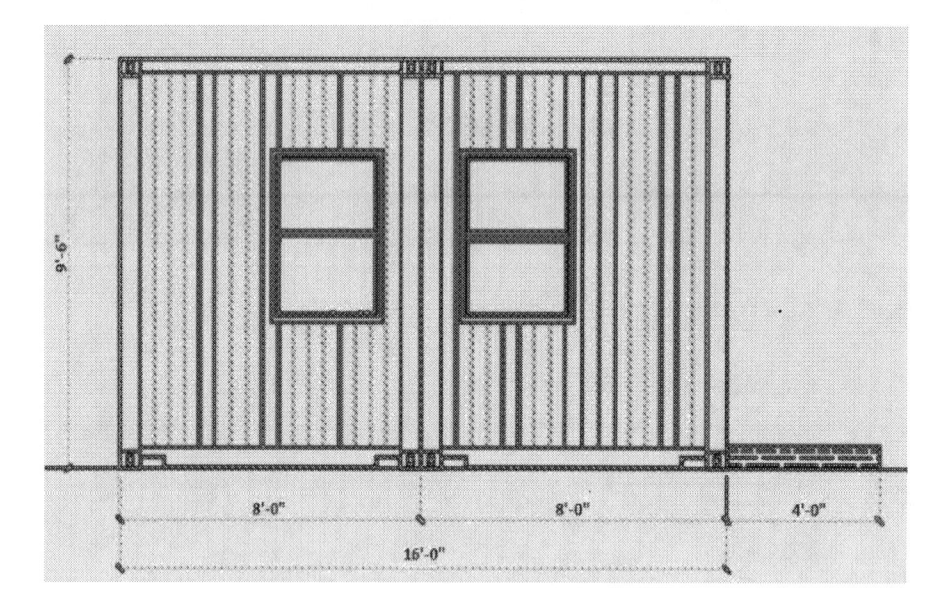

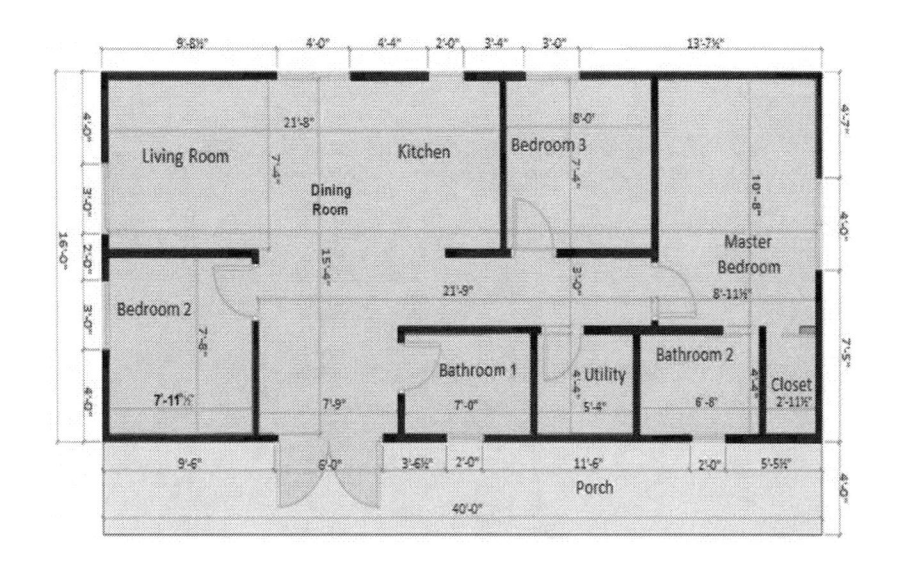

Plan 6 features 3 bedrooms and 2 bathrooms as well as a living room, dining room, kitchen, utility room, and closet. Ample living and storage space, all within 2 40 ft. containers. In addition, there is a full-length deck lining the front of the dwelling. With 606 sq. ft., this dwelling can comfortably house 3 adults or a family of 4.

Plan 7

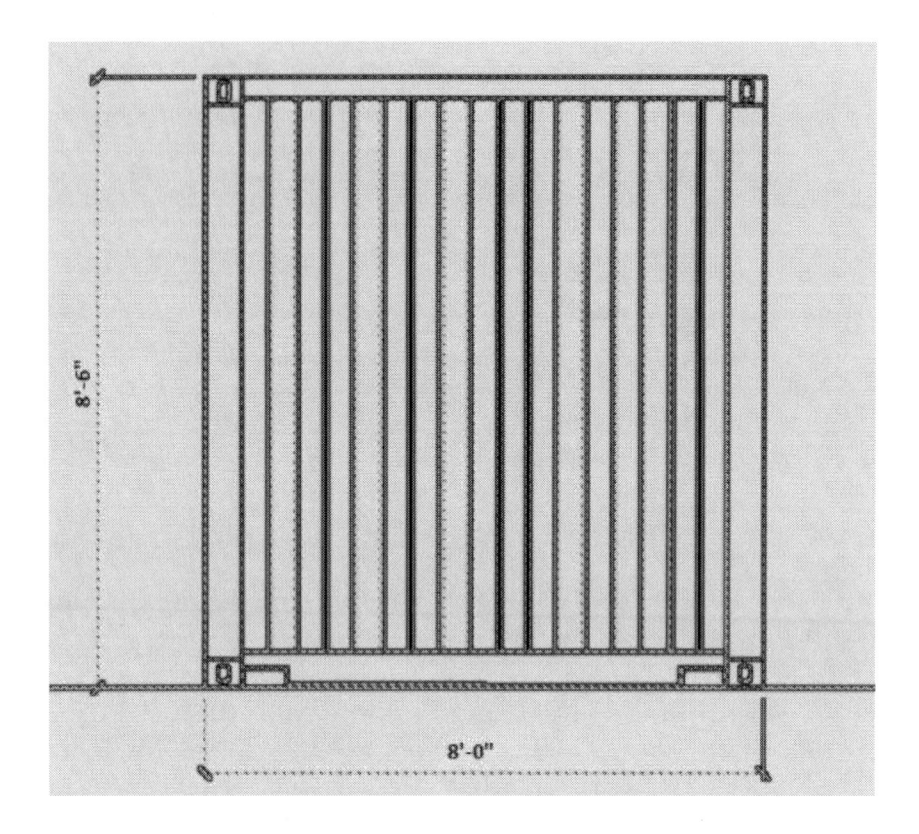

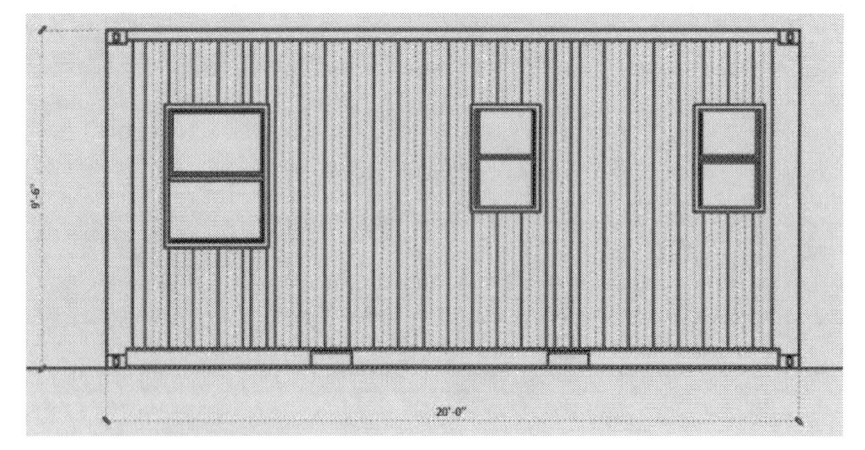

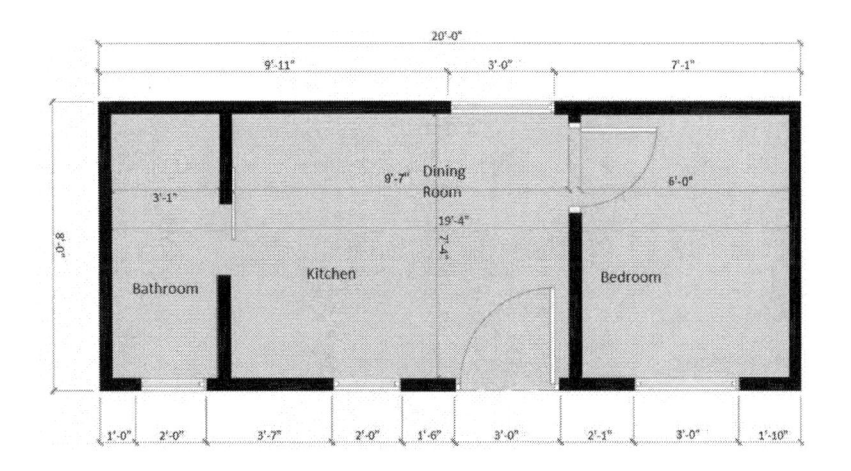

Plan 7 shows another design for a single 20 ft. container. This design combines spaciousness with efficiency, featuring a luxurious bathroom and master bedroom with a combined kitchen and dining room. This design is perfect for a single person or a couple, offering all the amenities necessary for a wilderness love nest within 135 sq. ft.

Plan 8

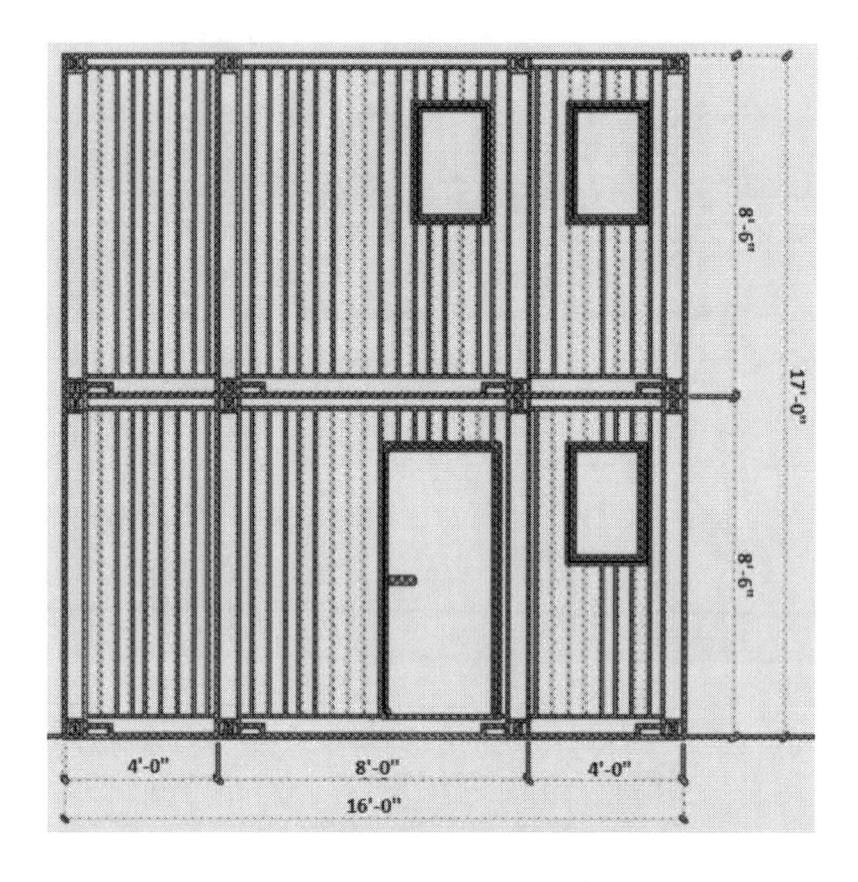

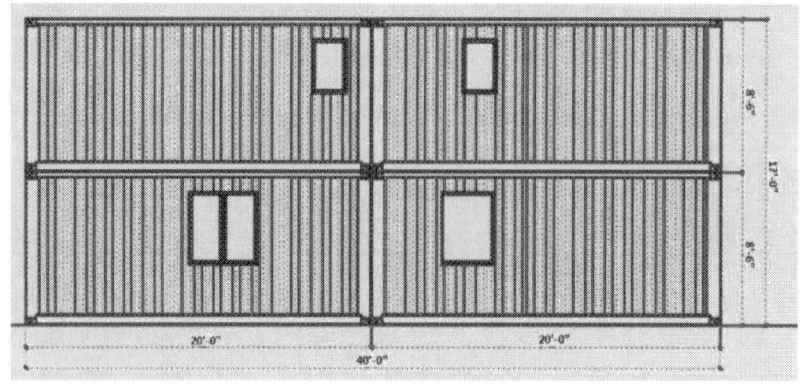

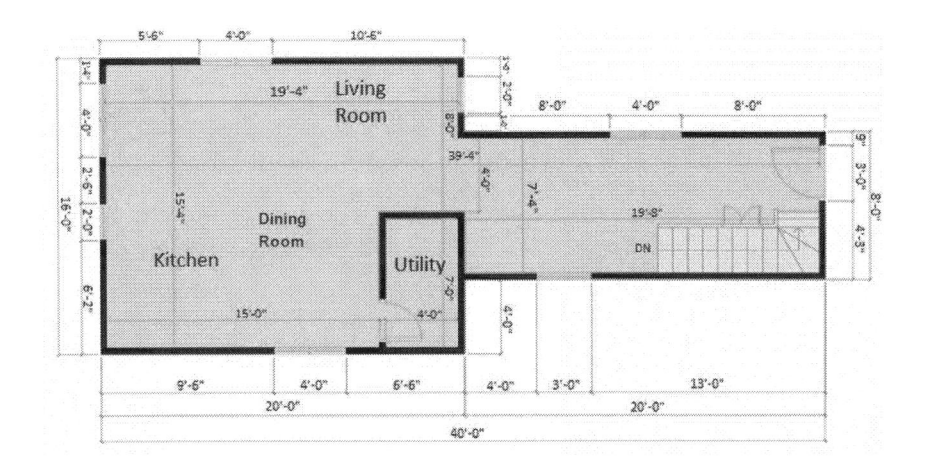

Upstairs:

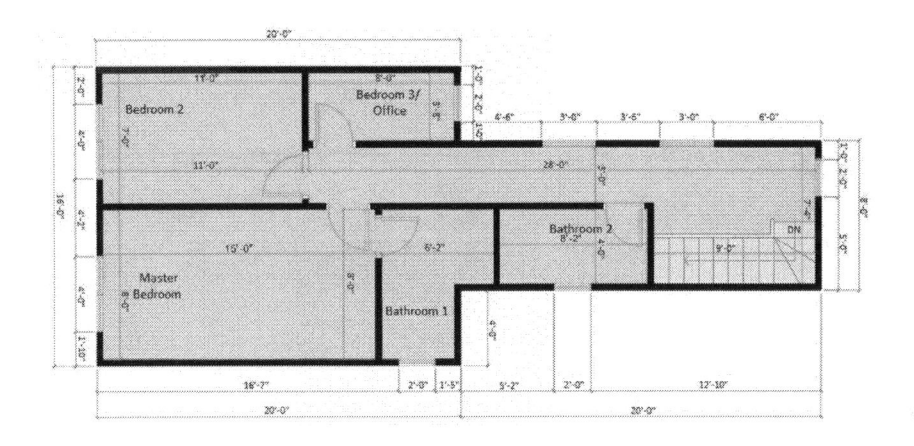

With 6 20 ft. containers and 861 sq. ft. of floor space, Plan 8 offers the utmost luxury. It features 3 bedrooms and 2 bathrooms on the upper floor, while the lower floor is devoted to a combined open-plan living room, dining room, and kitchen. Also included is a utility closet that serves your storage needs.

Plan 9

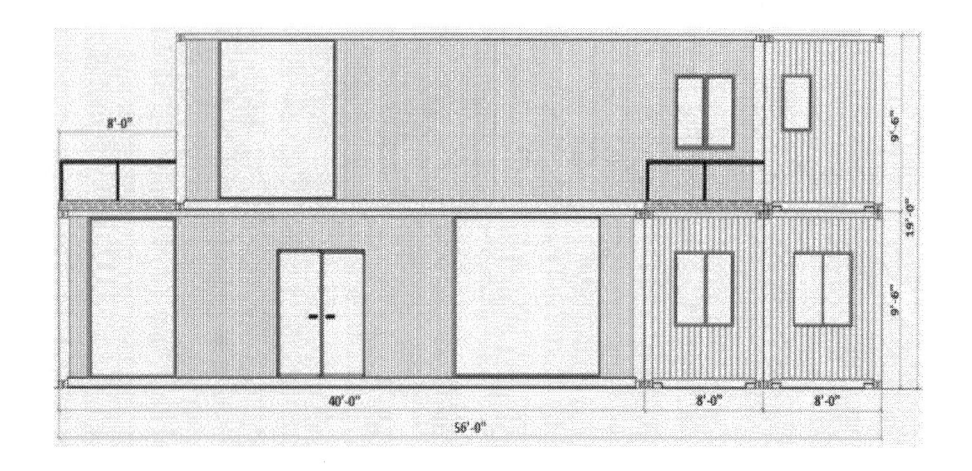

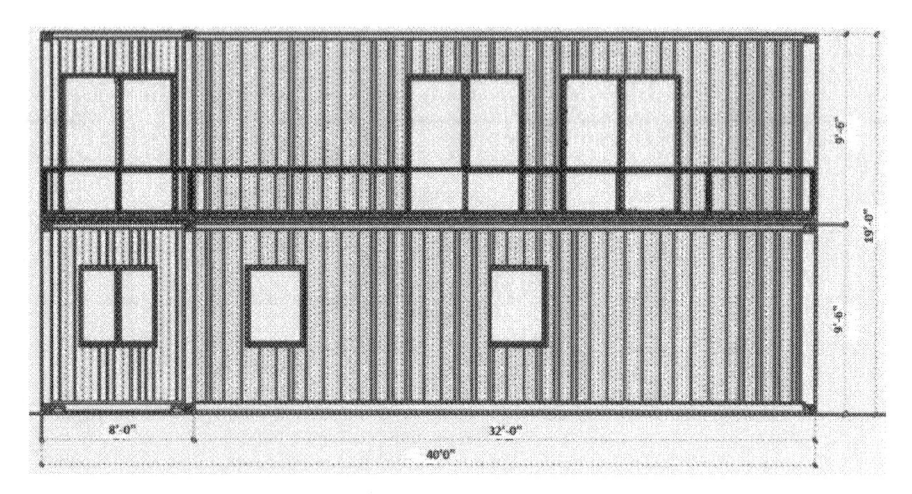

52

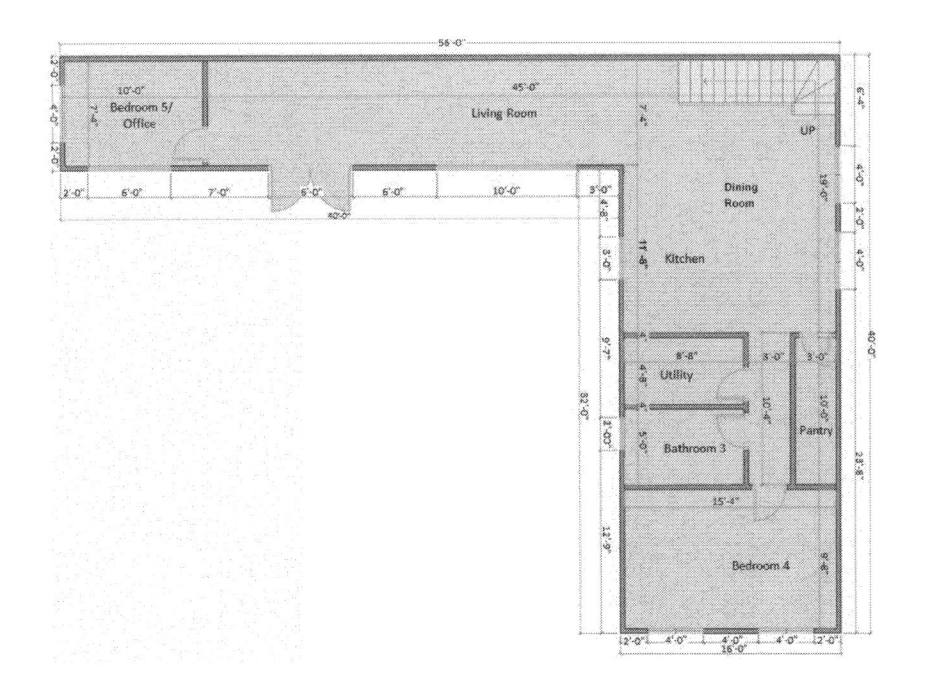

Upstairs:

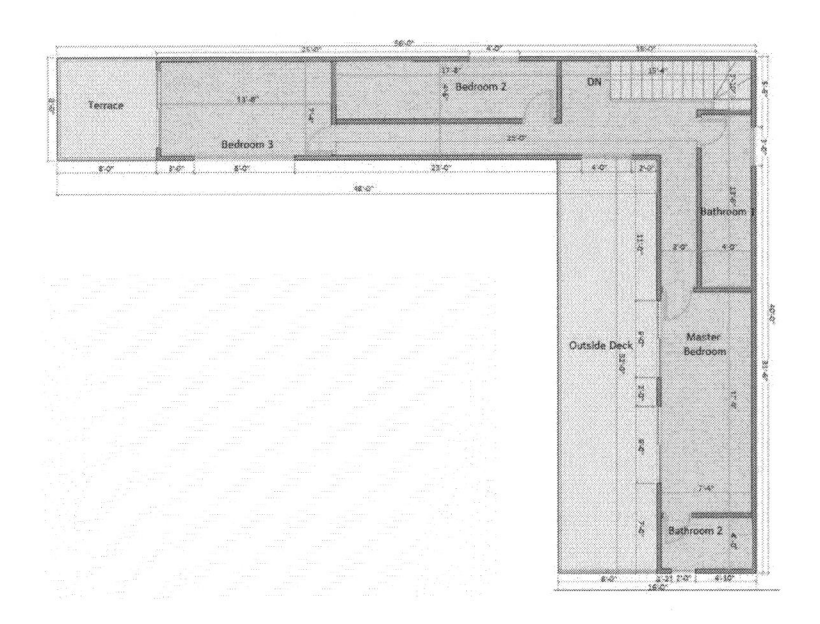

Plan 9 is composed of 5 40 ft. high cube containers and provides a total of 1718 sq. ft. of floor space. It houses 5 bedrooms and 3 bathrooms as well as a combined kitchen and dining room. Also includes a pantry and utility closet. The

53

second floor features an outside deck and terrace which are perfect for a combination of privacy and fresh air.

Plan 10

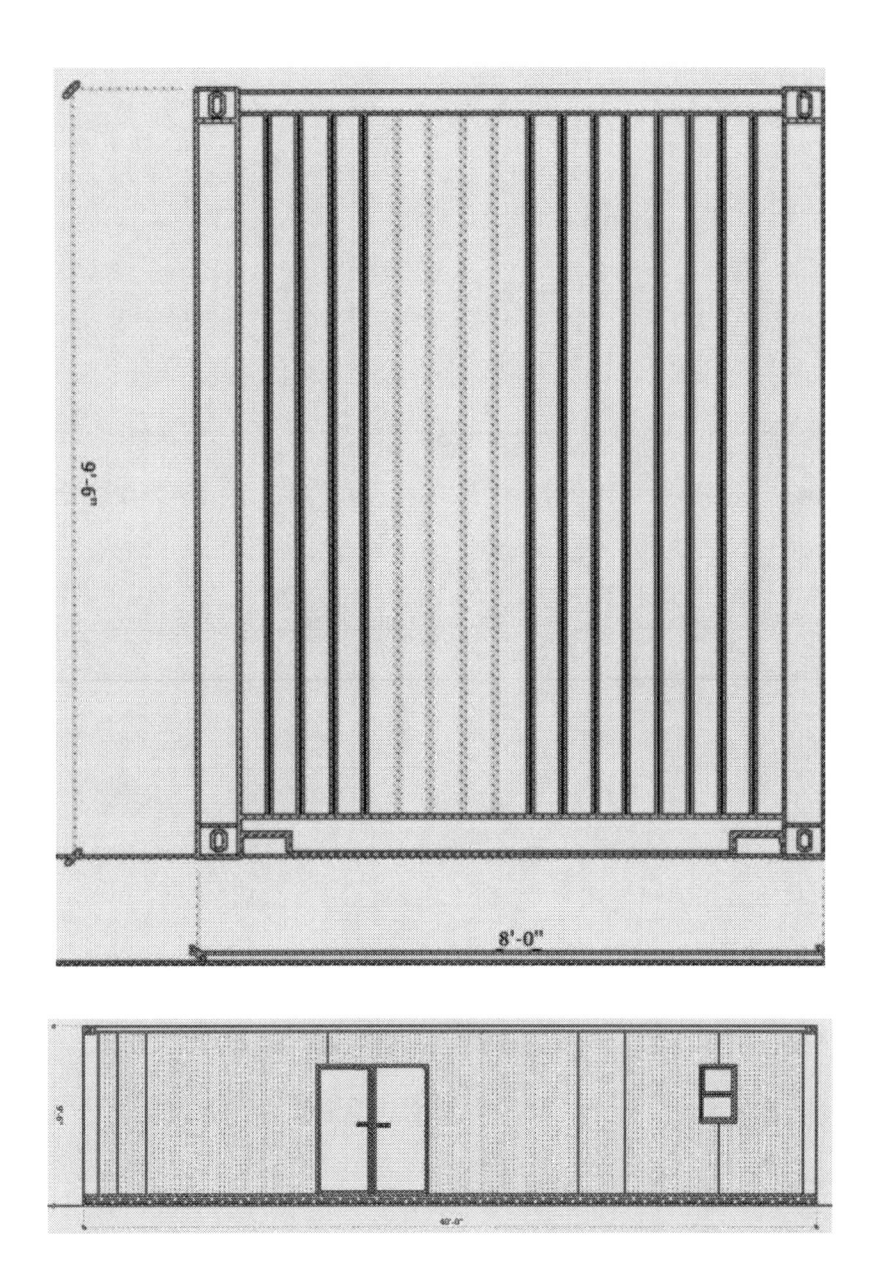

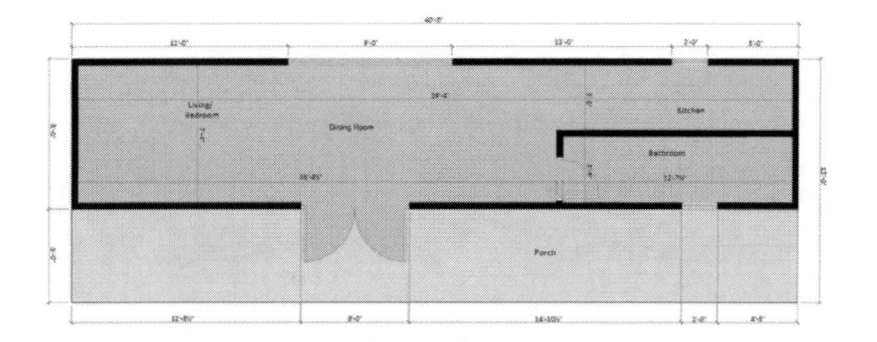

Constructed from a single 40 ft. container, Plan 10 offers a stunning 483 sq. ft. of floor space. It features a combined bedroom/living room and open-plan dining room, as well as a spacious bathroom and cozy kitchen. This design is ideal for 2 and can comfortably house 3 or more with a sofa bed.

Plan 11

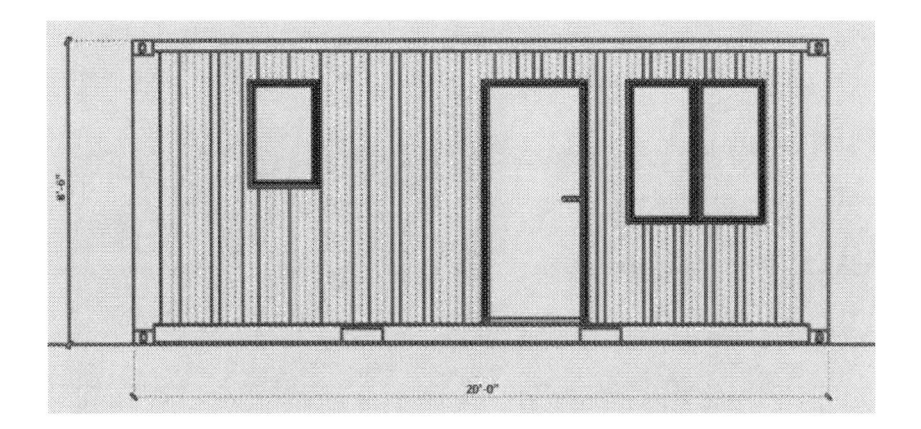

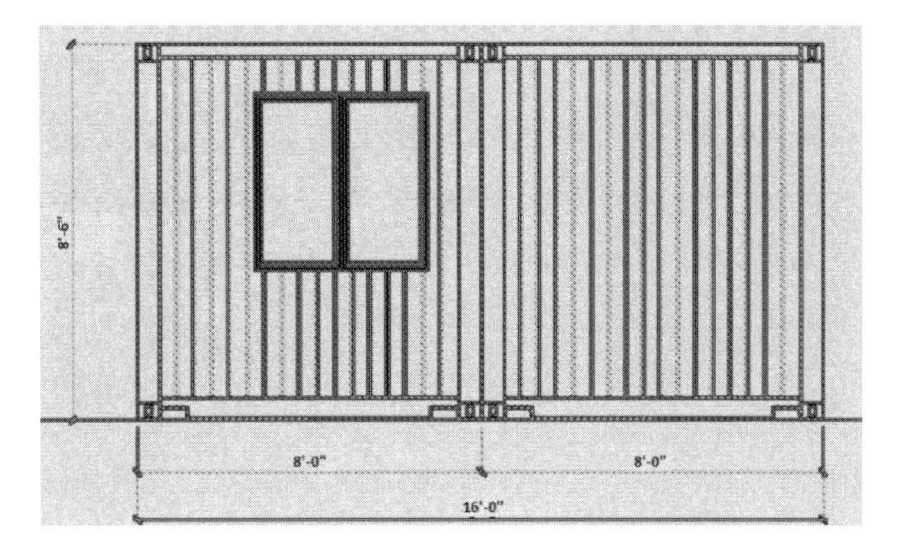

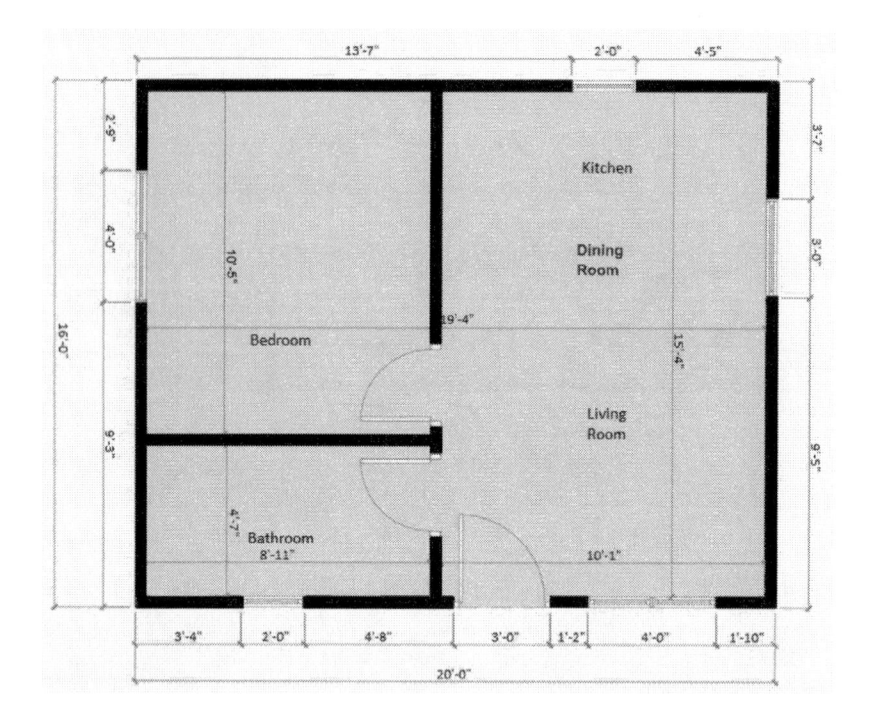

Made from only 2 20 ft. containers, Plan 11 offers 289 sq. ft. of floor space. It features a master bedroom, luxurious bathroom, and combined kitchen and dining room. The front door opens into an open-plan living room which is ideal for visitors, and which can be supplied with a sofa bed to comfortably house a second person.

Plan 12

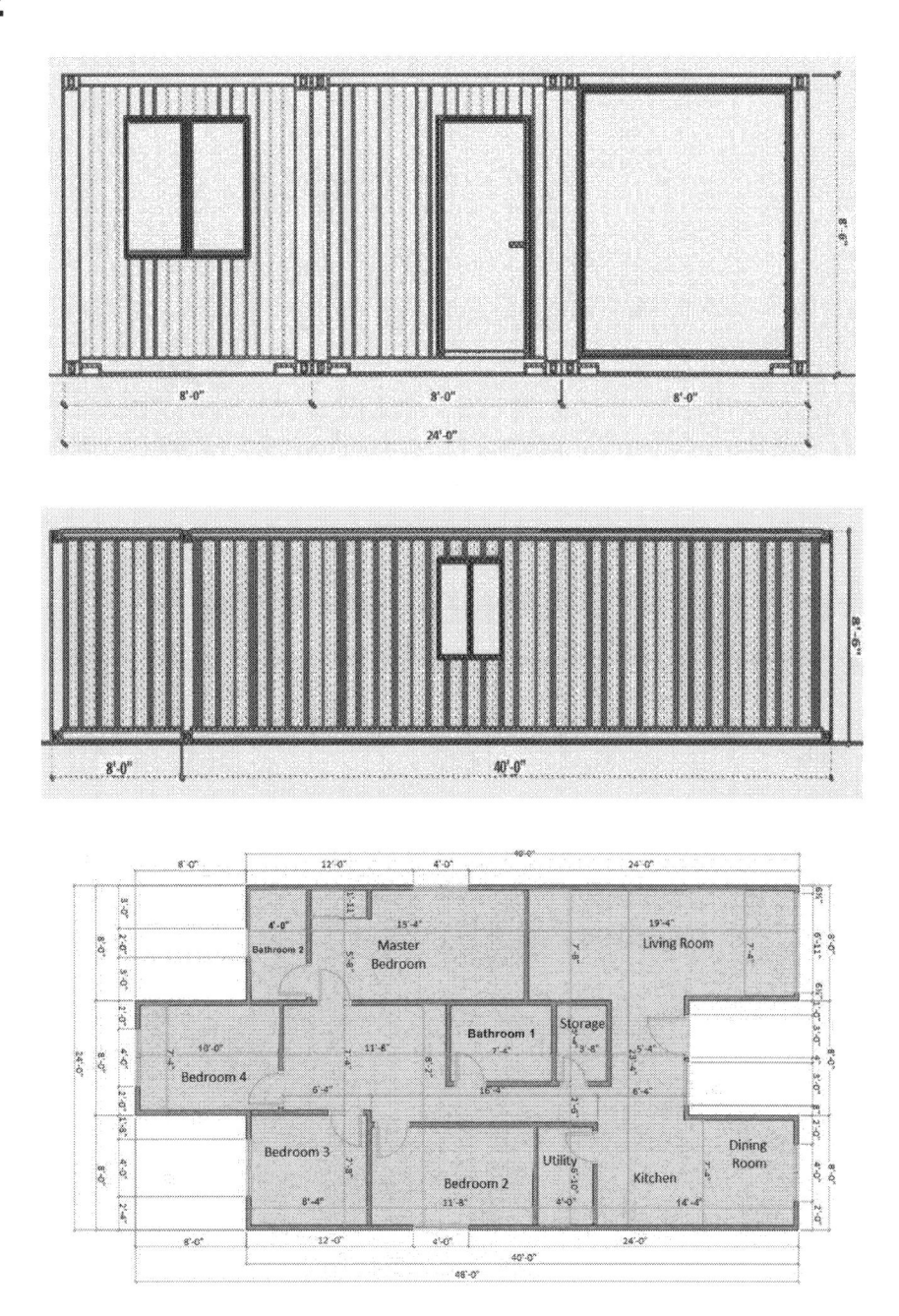

Constructed from merely 3 40 ft. containers, Plan 12 offers a spacious 899 sq. ft. of floor space. It features a master bedroom as well as 3 additional bedrooms and 2 bathrooms. It also has an efficiently combined dining room and

59

kitchen as well as a separate living room with ample space for entertaining visitors.

Plan 13

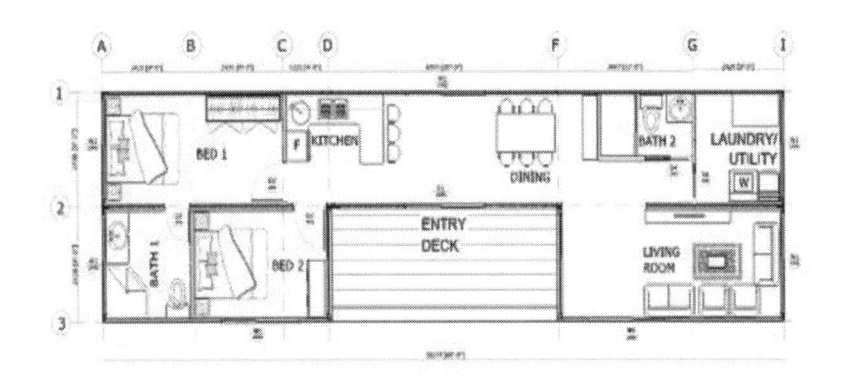

Above, you can see a U-shaped design, desired by those who like to have a deck. Doing this will certainly cut at the space you have inside; however, for many, this is a welcome sacrifice. This particular container was 40 ft., giving it the advantage of length to add to the interior space.

You can see how the container has been designed for 2 bedrooms, but both are quite small. The second bedroom is only about the size of the bed itself, not a place meant for relaxation. No room is spared for a closet or extra furniture. The second bathroom, too, is very small.

But is this necessarily a large sacrifice? After all, many houses, even large ones, keep their second or third bathroom very small half-baths. This is the bathroom for guests, after all, and if you already have a full bathroom near your bedroom, then what is the point of adding a second full one?

This floor plan also makes use of a separate living room and dining room. This means that, while the kitchen and dining areas are quite cramped, your living area is open and comfortable. Given that this is where most people spend their free time, along with the deck, it makes sense that more space would be dedicated to this area.

However, decks are not for everyone. If you live in a colder climate where you would make use of a deck perhaps 2 months out of a year, it doesn't make sense to sacrifice so much space for it. Have a look at the floor plan and replace the deck with space for something else.

But not everyone wants a 40 ft container. After all, they are much harder to move from place to place and to fit onto a certain plot of land. Take a look at the next 2 designs for what you can do with a more limited space of 20 ft.

Plan 14

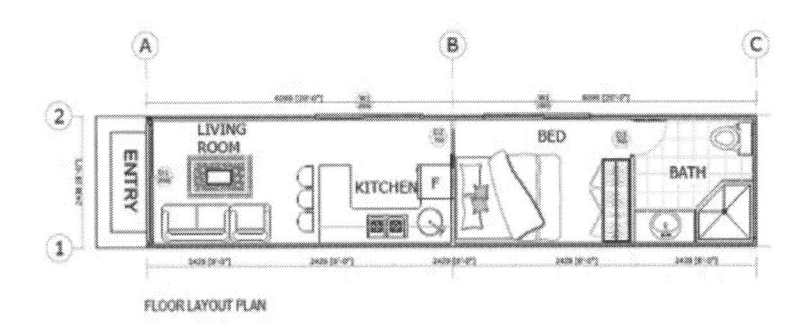

This is a smaller, 20 ft. container. It has rather the same layout as a trailer, with the living room close upon entry, and the bathroom far in the back. The caveat to a design like this is the bathroom factor. Any visitors who want to use the bathroom will have to pass through your bedroom. For some people, that's an invasion of privacy and not something easily handled.

So, consider, if this were your shipping container home, how you might rework it to move the bathroom somewhere else. Would you be willing to walk through a bathroom to get to your bedroom, if the positions were switched?

One nice thing about this plan is the use of an open concept floor space in the kitchen and living room. With such limited interior area as a shipping container gives, it is nice to leave rooms as wide open as they can, so you don't feel cramped in. Kitchens, especially, can feel cramped and overloaded because of all the cupboards, counters, and appliances that fill them. The open concept allows the kitchen to breathe a little more.

Plan 15

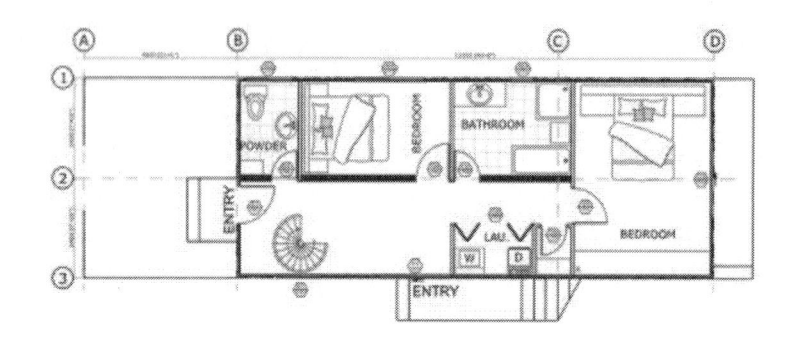

This plan has added a backdoor entrance, or in this case, more of a side door. It also includes a half bathroom in addition to the full bathroom and 2 bedrooms. One of the bedrooms is quite large. Likely, this is a plan for a second floor or an extra appendage to another house, but it is worth it to study as a single home nonetheless.

The extra bedroom and bathroom have taken up most of the space that would be used for a kitchen or living room, due to this being only a part of a larger whole. This is a good base to work off of if you want to practice redesigns. Replace the second bedroom and bathroom with a kitchen and living room. You might go with the open concept as with the last floor plan, and have your kitchen appliances along one wall while the living room spreads out across the floor. Or you could separate the kitchen as an entirely different room if you want to use more walls inside.

Notice, too, that this plan has left a lot of extra space in the bedroom. Though this does depend on you, bedrooms in micro houses and shipping container homes tend to be very small. However, plenty of people in this modern age are antisocial, introverted, or work from home by sitting in their own beds. For some of these people, you could completely forego a living room and just have your bedroom take up most of the space. Think of the way you live, now. If you rarely leave your bedroom on a normal day, is there really a point in separating the bedroom from the living space? We aren't even speaking of the old-fashioned Murphy beds that are pulled down from the walls, either. Put your bed in a room, with a desk, in front of the TV, with an armchair nearby and the kitchen only a few steps away. That is the true definition of cozy.

Plan 16

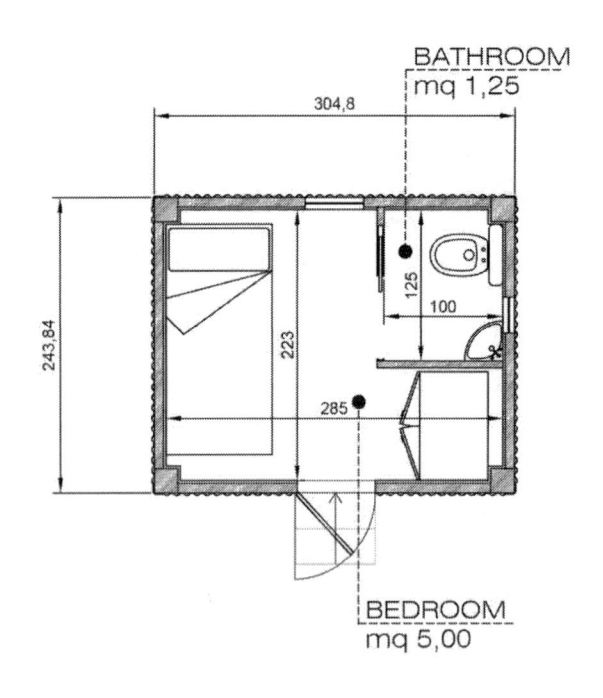

BATHROOM
mq 1,25

BEDROOM
mq 5,00

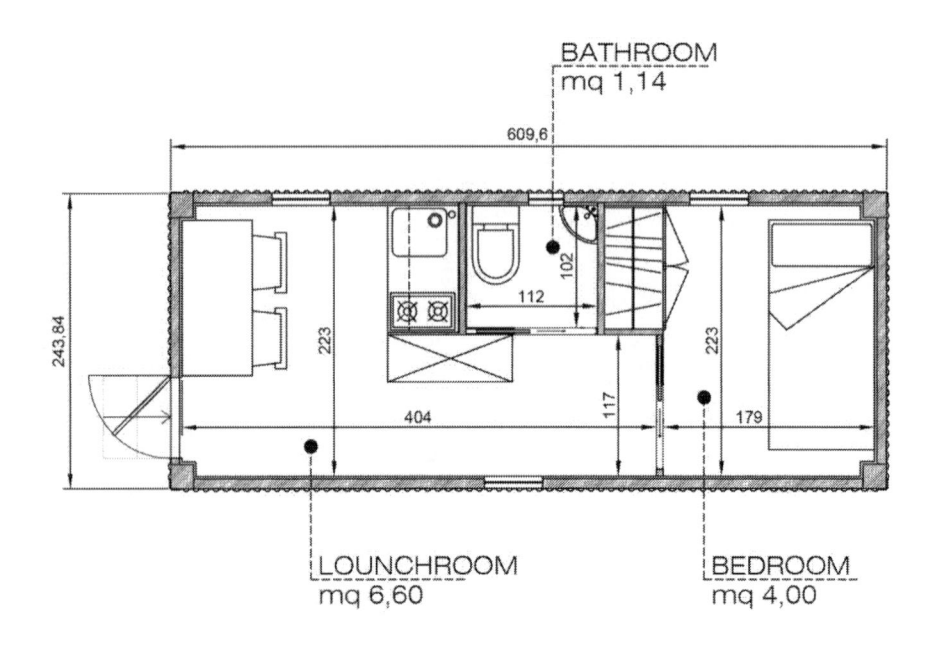

BATHROOM
mq 1,14

LOUNCHROOM
mq 6,60

BEDROOM
mq 4,00

This two-story model is minimalist in style yet functional. Dining room on the ground floor with kitchenette attached to the bathroom to take advantage of the same drainage systems. A single bedroom on the ground floor and one on the second floor provide cohabitation with maximum privacy. Ideal for singles or open couples. The presence of the two bathrooms also certainly provides adaptability for any guests.

The stairs are external and can be covered by a convenient canopy.

This container can also be thought of as a home/office. Changing the entrance door from the west side to the east side you can think of making the bedroom an office and use the second floor as a night home.

Plan 17

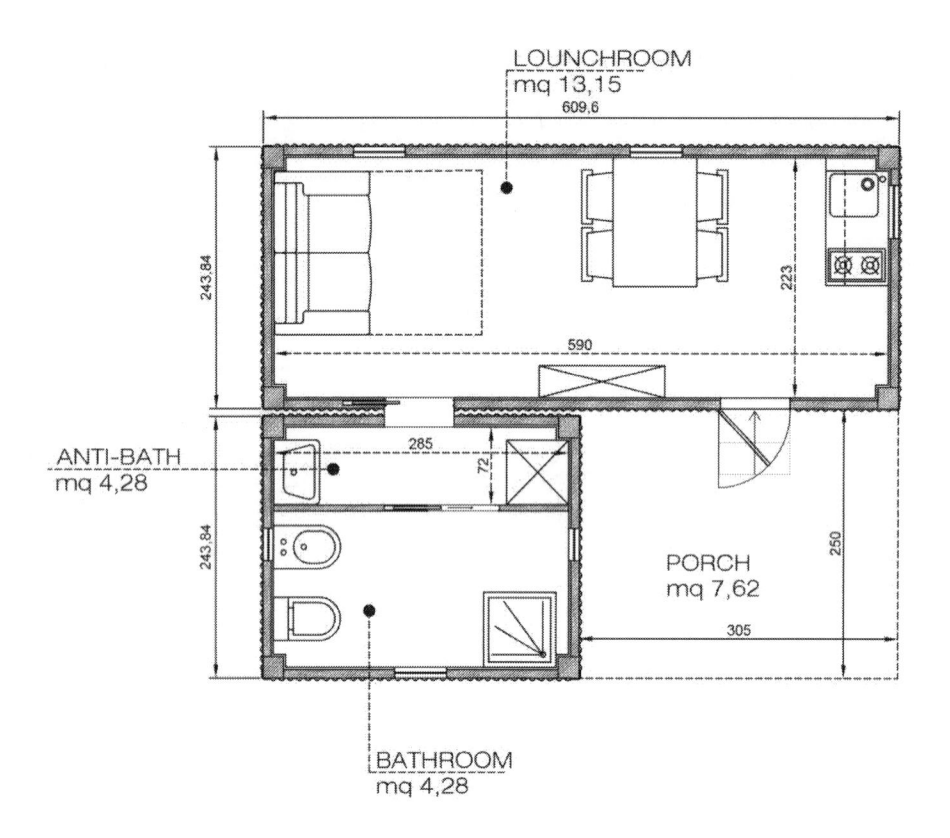

This solution offers multiple space advantages. In fact, the large dining room with comfortable sofa bed is great to have the comfort and intimacy of a real home, leaving also play space for any children. In addition, the huge bathroom with antechamber allows you to take advantage of the environment for real moments of relaxation.

In the model there is a shower box but it can be easily replaced with a custom-made bathtub.

In the periods of sunshine is also exploitable the porch where it can be installed a beautiful garden of real or fake grass where you can spend unforgettable moments or admire the surrounding landscape.

Plan 18

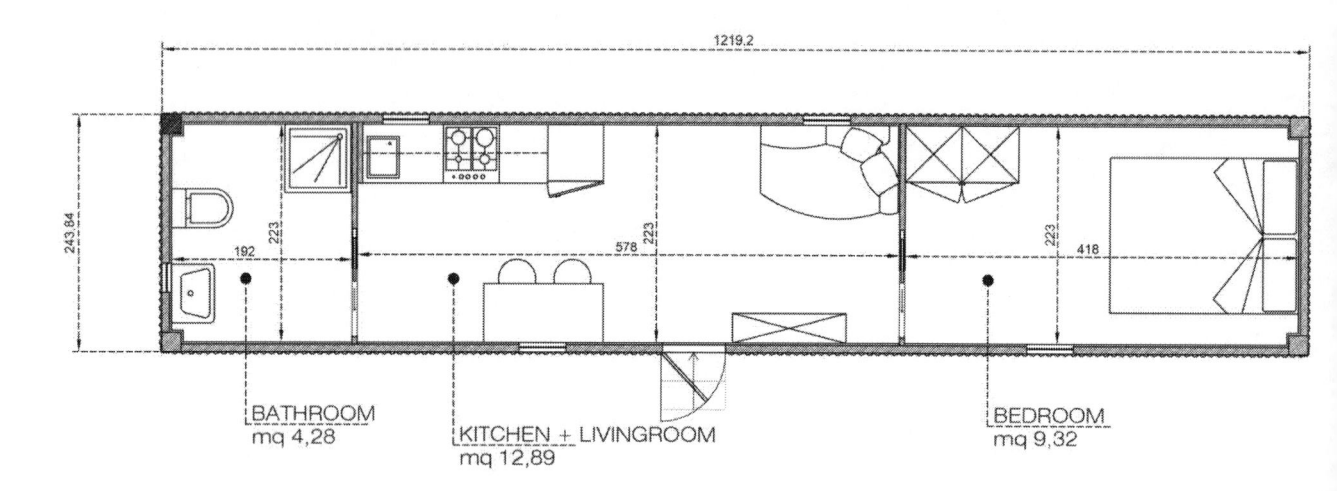

BATHROOM
mq 4,28

KITCHEN + LIVINGROOM
mq 12,89

BEDROOM
mq 9,32

The ideal solution for convenience! A dining room with a corner sofa and a respectable kitchen make for a warm, family-friendly environment.

An ideal living solution for couples also thanks to the large windowed bedroom.

Numerous points of light in the sides and strategic corners of the house, the structure suggests the use of the house in a comfortable and relaxing.

In addition, the bathroom of modest size is not only functional but also easy to clean.

Plan 19

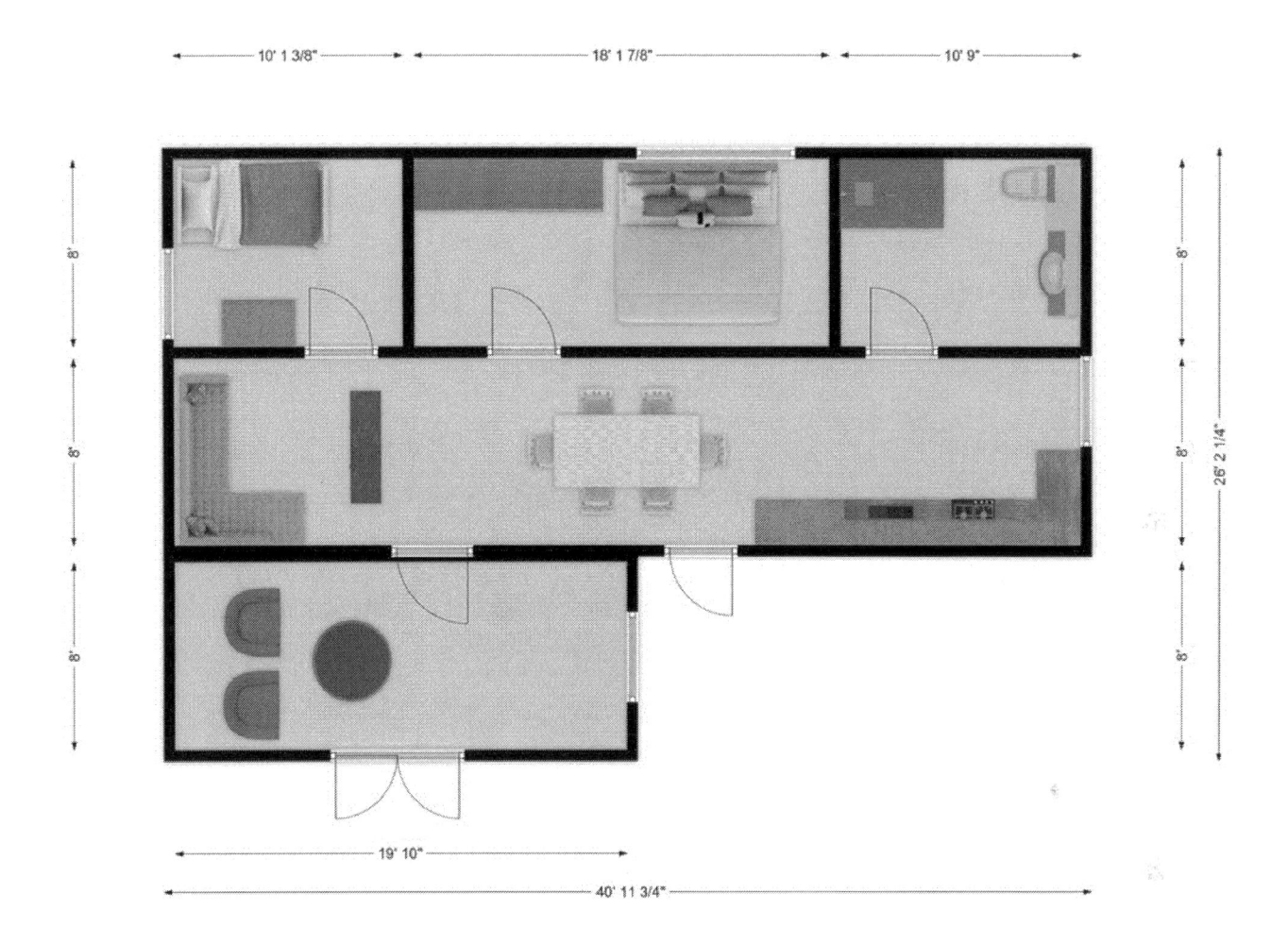

The true luxury home for those who invest in this type of housing. Spacious dining room with large kitchen and sofa. Well two bedrooms one double and one single. Full bathroom and small covered relaxation room with two armchairs and small tea table.

A real tiny-house for families complete with every comfort.

You enter from the relaxation room that already gives you the welcome you need to live a peaceful and tension-free life.

Easily you can imagine to live in such an environment taking advantage of all the spaces but leaving the right one to breathe the desire of family.

Plan 20

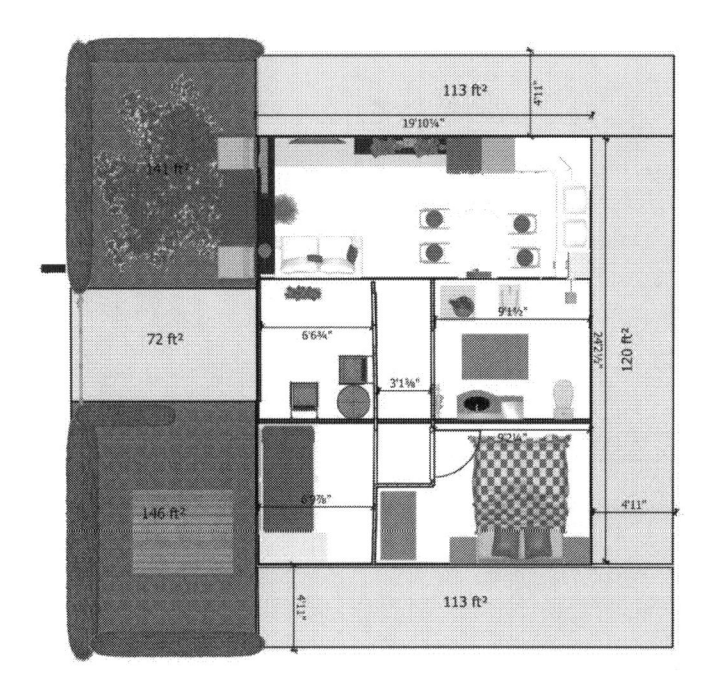

This floor plan is definitely the best idea for your dream home. There is truly everything here. Comfortable bathroom, two bedrooms, dining room with very large kitchen and sofa and even outdoor open space with large fenced garden that can be used for wonderful Sunday barbecues.

The layout of the rooms also allows you to create a space to exclude the smells of the kitchen from the bedroom and keep the air fresh and clean even for colder winters.

Here you truly appreciate the comfort of a self-built home and can adapt it to your taste and needs as you see fit.

Chapter 6.   Foundation

Before you can place your container, you'll need to prepare some form of foundation. This will provide a stable, level surface for the container to sit on. While there are 3 suitable types of foundations not all local authorities will accept all 3 and you may have no choice but to use a certain type only. Ideally, you'll want a qualified expert and engineer to lay your foundations as they will know how to deal with soil, codes, and the land topography itself. The 3 main types used for container homes are pile, raft, and concrete pier foundations. This is another area where you don't want to compare the shipping container to a mobile home as they are usually much heavier which requires a different type of reinforcement in the concrete.

The two most important considerations when laying a foundation are cost and structure. Structurally you need to consult a professional as they will know best about distributing the weight of your container. With softer soil, your foundation needs to be deeper as this adds more stability while hard soil or rock may only require leveling and minor foundation work. There's a tendency to over-spec foundations too which means making them stronger than is strictly necessary simply for peace of mind.

Concrete Piers

These are often similar to what is used for shed and small outbuildings, and they're often the cheapest type of foundation because they require the least materials. In the most basic these are concrete piers that contain reinforced steel bars that are placed strategically. The steel bars or occasionally steel mesh add to the stability and strength of the concrete. If you are planning on DIYing the foundation this is the easiest way to go because it requires the least concrete and least scientific approach. These piers should be placed anywhere that the 'load' or main weight of the containers will be—the middle and the corners generally. If you're placing more than one container together you may want to place additional piers at the seams of the two so that both are fully supported. An average of 6 piers per container is standard.

Slab-on-Grade

Raft foundation is significantly more expensive but it's more stable than piers, the reason for this is that the entire container is supported on a concrete raft rather than perched. However, it also requires some digging into the topsoil. The raft foundation is still quite quick to build and is a better idea where temperatures don't drop below freezing much as this lower ground temperature can affect the concrete. It also means that the concrete is prone to getting cold and allowing heat to leach away from your container which is why it's not ideal for cold climates since this will drive up your heating bill. The slab is less affected by bugs and termites as well since there's no wood involved. However, if you're planning on using a slab foundation you MUST have your utilities embedded into the slab and the connections placed exactly to connect with those inside the container since there will be no access to them once the concrete has been set and no way to lay them afterward.

Pile Foundation

Similar to concrete piers these are deeper and more structurally challenging which is why they tend to be the most expensive. This is the type of foundation necessary when your soil is weak and not suitable for a solid slab. There's a great design study with a container home using these called the Graceville Container Home Study which centered around a family whose original home was devastated by flooding and they needed a cheaper rebuilding alternative. Their home was a 3-layer 6000 ft. design that featured everything from a pool and gym to a studio. They needed the deeper piles because of the flood and cyclone risk.

The piles are solid cylindrical steel tubes that are hammered down until they are in more solid ground. Once they are secured they are filled with concrete and steel rebar which resembles the same as the piers above ground. This is not a construction that can be done DIY because of the need for a pile driver. Since this is the most secure, it is recommended to use this type of foundation, anyway if you are doing a multiple stacked design as it will provide extra support.

Strip Foundation

Less common is a combination of slab and pier, known as strip foundations. These are strips of thick concrete laid out either on part of the container footprint or around the whole thing. This is a cheaper alternative than a slab but more stable than piers. This is a good choice when the ground is wetter as the inside area being open allows for better drainage. They are, however, less stable than a pile foundation and prone to slippage in high winds or earthquakes since the container can slide. They're quite shallow as well which means they're not suited for stacked container designs.

Concrete Foundation

Concrete comes in many grades, and if you've ever looked at the hardware store, you'll see many different types. When it comes to building a foundation, you'll need to use a specific strength of concrete based on your land. The strength is measured in C with a number after it; the higher the number the stronger the concrete. C15 is general-purpose concrete while C30 is a much stronger concrete. C15 uses 1 part cement to 2 parts of sand and 5 gravel, the amount of cement used increases the strength of the concrete. It's easy to mix small amounts by hand but for piers and slabs you will need a concrete mixer or to order ready-mix delivered. This does increase the cost of your concrete but it ensures that you don't have one chunk of concrete already dried while you're still mixing it. You must mix it properly together so that it is thoroughly combined or you risk having different structural densities which can cause cracks and weaken over time.

Calculating the amount of concrete needed is fairly simple, you need to know how many square feet your concrete area covers and then mix accordingly. For a 20 ft. container, for example, if you were placing it on a raft foundation that was 2 ft. deep and just wider than the container you would want an area that was 10'x22'x2' or 440 cubed ft. of concrete.

When the concrete is mixed it begins a curing process that eventually hardens and sets it. This typically takes between 5–7 days and requires some moisture to be added to prevent it from drying out too quickly on top and cracking.

During the curing period, the weather and temperature need to remain fairly constant and both extreme hot and cold can affect the curing process.

In hot weather, you'll need some form of shade to protect it from direct sunlight and the ground should be sprayed with cold water before pouring. The concrete itself should be mixed with cold water and if possible laid in the evening or early morning to avoid the heat of the day.

In cold weather (below 0°C for 3 consecutive days), make sure any frost or standing water is cleared from the foundation area first. Then lay the concrete and cover it with an insulating blanket layer immediately. The blankets should remain on for the entire curing time before being removed gradually to raise the temperature slowly and prevent cracking.

Footings

Soil Bearing Capacities	
Class of Materials	Load-Bearing Pressure (pounds per square foot)
Crystalline bedrock	12,000
Sedimentary rock	6,000
Sandy gravel or gravel	5,000
Sand, silty sand, clayey sand, silty gravel, and clayey gravel	3,000
Clay, sandy clay, silty clay, and clayey silt	2,000
Source: Table 401.4.1; CABO One- and Two- Family Dwelling Code; 1995.	

Within the concrete, you will need footings. These are there to support the foundation and prevent it from settling unevenly and cracking. These are essentially the 'feet' that your foundation rests on and are usually 16–20 inches wide. These are better in good load-bearing soil but if your soil has an uneven distribution you may have to place different footings across your foundation to make sure it stays solid. When the footing isn't centered properly or the ground is uneven the weight of the building above pushes down and will eventually cause the footing to give way, making the foundation crack. This is almost always determined by an engineer, and even they sometimes get it wrong. The footings are tied very strongly to the type of soil and its bearing capacity.

Footings should be placed a minimum of 6 inches below where the frost line in the ground is. When the earth freezes it shifts slightly which means that a footing placed above this line will move with temperature changes.

The average footing comes in one of 3 sizes (plus frost line depth):

- 8 x 16 x 16 inches
- 12 x 24 x 24 inches
- 10 x 20 x 20 inches

Each footing is constructed separately usually starting with those which are higher if the design is leveling a slope. The footings are made using ½ inch rebar which is 8 inches longer than the depth of the concrete. Once the footing hole is dug the rebar is driven or hammered into the ground so that the top of the rebar is level with the intended top of the concrete. The rebar should be placed every few inches and the amount of rebar will depend on how big your footings are.

Minimum Width of Concrete or Masonry Footings (inches)

	Load-Bearing Value of Soil (psf)					
	1,500	2,000	2,500	3,000	3,500	4,000
Conventional Wood Frame Construction						
1-story	16	12	10	8	7	6
2-story	19	15	12	10	8	7
3-story	22	17	14	11	10	9
4-Inch Brick Veneer Over Wood Frame or 8-Inch Hollow Concrete Masonry						
1-story	19	15	12	10	8	7
2-story	25	19	15	13	11	10
3-story	31	23	19	16	13	12
8-Inch Solid or Fully Grouted Masonry						
1-story	22	17	13	11	10	9
2-story	31	23	19	16	13	12
3-story	40	30	24	20	17	15

Source: Table 403.1; *CABO One- and Two- Family Dwelling Code*; 1995.

While this table is intended on applying to a standard construction the load-bearing values compared to the heaviest construction will give you an idea of the expected bearing of each footing. Sometimes your footings aren't perfect and if it is off-center in good soil it may not be a problem, however, if the footing isn't centered correctly for the foundation it will need to be fixed either using gravel, an additional steel tie, or re-augmenting the footing.

If you find you have a soft spot, one where the rebar simply disappears, you may need to excavate and create a pile for that specific footing rather than a pier construction. An alternative is to excavate the soft soil completely and fill the hole back in with gravel or a lower grade concrete. You cannot simply increase the width of the footing without changing the thickness which can cause the concrete to crack.

In fact, there's so much potential that needs to be correct about footings on its own that it could fill a book.

Fixing the Container

Whichever foundation you have chosen you'll need a solid way of attaching the container. The steel plate should have vertical bars that sink into the concrete and will add stability. After the curing process has finished the container can be welded directly onto these steel plates. The plates should be a minimum of 1/4 to 1/2 inch thick, with thicker plates being stronger. You will still see the top of the plate and this needs to be level across the entire foundation. There are some local codes that apply to this when it comes to metal plates and grades for attachment screws so it's good to do some research if you're DIYing.

An alternative to welding plates is simply to bolt the container directly into the concrete with anchors. This is much simpler and cheaper; however, it is not as strong. You can also use J hooks to attach the container to the exposed rebar in the concrete directly. Concrete anchors are the weakest choice but they can also be an added safety measure if you do these and plate welding.

There is no hard rule about fixing the container to the foundation, and if you're planning on potentially moving the container at a later date you may choose not to. There is nothing wrong with simply placing the container on top of the foundation but there is a distinct lack of stability and this may affect your home insurance at a later date if it's found to be a factor with damage. Welding makes the containers much harder to remove if you want your home to be portable.

Chapter 7.   Receiving Container

Most important, you have a certain design in mind, and all that is left is for you to get the shipping containers you have selected, and you can get to work. Before we get to that, you need to understand your options for working on the container on site. Do you want to receive the container as it is, work on it yourself to cut through the walls, and install the windows and such? Or would you prefer a prefab container? Another option is working on it off-site, which means you will have a factory work on your specs and then it will be delivered to you ready to go.

Prefab Containers

Everything that needs to happen to the container will take place in the workshop before it is delivered to you. The great thing about this option is that it saves a lot of time and effort, and the containers delivered to you will be ready to be directly placed on the foundation you had set earlier. It also might save you money in the long run, because if you DIY, you might permanently damage the container and cost yourself extra repair money, or worse, be forced to replace it altogether.

On the other hand, if the containers are prefabricated, they are converted to the shape and condition you need with no effort. A cool feature you get with prefab services is that they often have deals with installation services, so you won't have to worry about installing a heavy container yourself or moving it from the workshop to your site. With prefab containers, you will get someone to install the container and connect them however you like, plus secure their placement so they don't fall off. Yes, this is expensive, but it is still cheaper compared to a traditional home.

On-Site Conversion

With on-site conversions, you will be doing most of the work yourself to create the home's shell that will be your living space. This includes everything from cutting walls to making arches and windows through the steel. You will obviously need a lot of equipment like blowtorches, sturdy drills, grinders, and a lot more. With this DIY approach, you will be saving yourself a lot of money since there aren't any additional shipping costs (if you shipped to a workshop) and you won't have to pay for labor or the machinery they use.

Another great advantage of on-site conversion is that you work on your own schedule; you can work at night, early mornings, or on weekends. You aren't bound by any workers' schedules with on-site conversion, which can prove quite useful and easy. On-site conversion is safer since you will do all the work on the container and it will already be on site. Changing the container structure often weakens its structural integrity a little, which isn't problematic if it is already at its resting place. But if you are moving it, this might lead to problems. With on-site conversion, you won't have to worry about shipping it to your location and you can avoid any accidents that might happen to the container along the road.

The biggest challenge with on-site conversion, though, is that it is difficult. You need to have a certain skill set and the necessary tools to take on such a task. If you don't have the equipment needed, you must buy it, making this more costly than other conversion options. There's also the problem with having access to power and supply in a site that might not have any yet since you might not yet have any utilities. This means you will need a generator—another significant expense if you don't already have one.

Naturally, there's the predicament of noise and the neighbors' disturbance if you are in a busy neighborhood.

While you can hire contractors to convert the containers on-site, this will be a more expensive option compared to a DIY approach. At least this way, you won't have to worry about not having the right tools for the job or the required set of skills to do it right. This is also a better option if you can't find a local workshop to do the work on your container.

Off-Site Conversion

The last option you have to convert containers is off-site conversion. While this option is also great if you don't have the necessary tools or experience/skills to take on this task, it has its downsides as well. However, offsite conversion is great if you don't want to bother with working on making the adjustments yourself. The good news is you will have experienced professionals doing all the work, so you won't have to worry about the experience factor here. Offsite conversion can be done by you as well. You can have the container delivered to a local workshop or fabricator and work there. They'd have the necessary tools to help you, and you will also get help if you run into any roadblocks.

Another perk of offsite conversion is that your container will be kept safe. The last thing you need is for your container to get soaking wet or suffer from any other unexpected weather conditions like snow while it's being modified, which could easily happen with on-site conversion. If your container is delivered to a workshop, it will be stored under a roof or indoors if there are any weather complications, so it will be protected. Dealing with a workshop—whether you will do the work yourself or have someone there do it for you—is also useful because there will be electricity on-site, so there won't be a reason for you to worry about electricity and getting a generator.

On the other hand, there is always the concern that something might happen to the container after the modifications and during transport to the site. Remember: the container is more fragile after conversion. The workshop location might present difficulties as well; it may be far away, creating a long commute for you, regardless of whether you want to do the work yourself every day or just oversee it. Also, consider that you won't be working at your own schedule; the workshop has working hours that might not suit you or might present a problem, but you must abide by those hours (ask about working hours before you sign off with any workshop).

Shipping

With your modifications in mind and the site prepared, all that remains is delivering the container so you can get to work. While that sounds easy, it might present a few complications. For starters, where are you going to get your container from? How much does it cost?

Buy Local

Many shipping container buyers mistakenly look at the container's price without taking shipping into consideration. Plus, shipping containers from other countries are risky and might get damaged on the way and arrive in a different shape than what you've seen online.

Buying local also makes it easier since the dealer can help ensure that you get all your containers from the same company and of similar quality. Generally, it is a good idea to look around and examine several options. Don't settle for the first few containers you come across—there might be better deals just around the corner.

Cost

Usually, shipping rates are fixed and are calculated for a standard distance of 50 miles. For a 20 ft. container, the shipping rates would be around $200–$250 for transporting and offloading. Distances farther than 50 miles will entail a fee per mile, around $2/mile for the total distance. If the container is 40 ft., prices are almost double that. So, it's $400–$500 for 50 miles. Prices may vary depending on the shipping company and its rates and policies. You can find a shipping company offering a flat rate for a total distance greater than 50 miles for a 20 or 40 ft. container, so, shop around.

Plan Ahead

Plan ahead for container shipping and delivery. You need to be around for when the container arrives so you can receive them and place them, and you don't want the shipping company to deliver them in your absence. You need to get the details of the delivery right. Some people order the container before they prepare the site in an attempt to save time. You might get the containers earlier than expected, and the soil is not ready yet. What would you do then?

Don't take any chances with container delivery. Make sure the site is ready and the conversion plan is set, and order your container at a time you are certain you can receive them, and the site will be ready. Details make a lot of difference here. If you plan on insulating the bottom of your container, the insulating material needs to be ready so you can get to work right away. Pay attention to those small details because they distinguish between a successful delivery and a lot of complications you don't need.

Container Placement

You will need to place the container on your selected foundation so you can work on the shell of your home. Once the container reaches the site, you will have a couple of different approaches to place it, but you need to do it slowly and carefully.

Tilting

The first approach to properly placing the container is to tilt it into place. To do that, you will need to have it moved on a flatbed trailer, which is an option that won't cost you a lot of money. Then, assuming it is possible to do this on the site, you will ask the driver to tilt the trailer's bed so the container can slide smoothly on the foundation.

Cranes

Your second option is using a crane. This is ideal for sites without any wiggle room for the truck driver to tilt the container, and also this is how to go if you plan on stacking a couple of containers over one another because tilting won't be much good then. While cranes are a more expensive option that entails renting the machine, paying for its operational cost and the labor operating it, they are very efficient and do the job quickly and with no complications. Remember to take the size/weight of your container into consideration because there are different types of cranes and some might not be able to lift 40 ft.

containers. Ask first, ensuring that you get the right piece of equipment for the job.

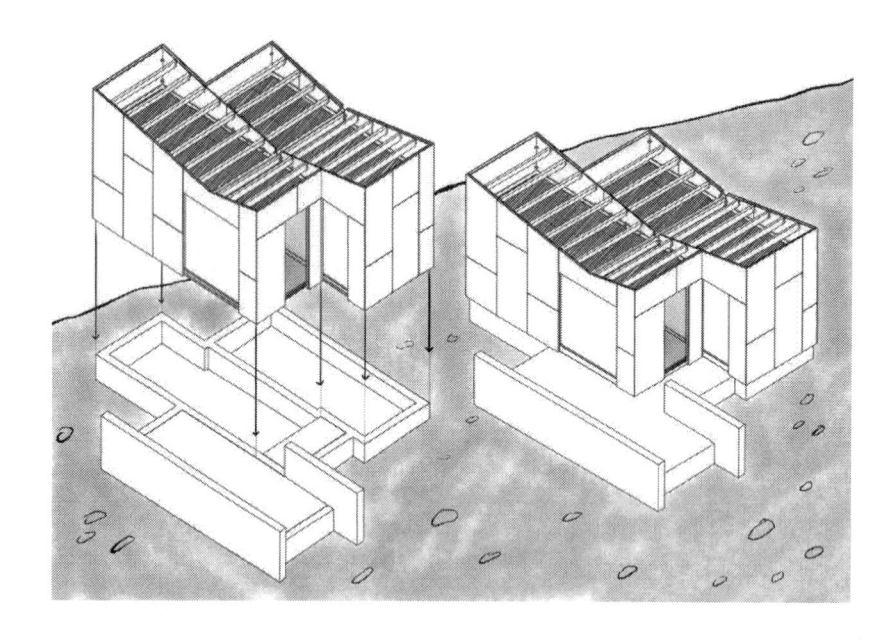

Assembly of ready-made containers on a concrete base.

Note: The foundation surface needs to be completely level before you can place the container. If you place the container on an uneven foundation, you must use shims and spaces to bring the container level; this complicates things. So, as much as you can, level the foundation's surface before you place the container on it.

Also, remember to add insulation to the underside of the container between it and the foundation. We talked earlier about the different options you get with insulation, and this is when you first need to apply that knowledge. Insulating the container's underside helps you control the temperature, which comes not just from the walls. After insulating the bottom, you can work your way to the interior of the container.

Anchoring the Containers

For safety reasons, a shipping container needs to be anchored so you can be 100% certain that it is at no risk of overturning or tilting due to unexpected weather conditions. Studies show that anchoring the container can help it withstand winds up to 150 miles per hour. Anchoring also helps minimize the chances of any damage happening due to settlement. There are different ways to anchor your shipping container, and it will depend on several factors, starting with the type of foundation you have.

Welding

This is one of the best ways to anchor a shipping container and it always yields great results and provides excellent stability. We mentioned earlier the importance of adding steel plates when you pour the concrete of your foundation, and this is where those plates come in handy. After your foundation, say piers, cures and the concrete harden, you can weld the container to the steel plate. This helps create a resilient foundation that can withstand just about anything, and it significantly increases the overall durability of your shipping container home.

Generally, it is optimal to weld the container at the adjoining parts of the roof, floors, and walls. Use flat steel at those points and stitch weld, leaving no spaces between containers. Any areas where the overlapping occurs need to be properly welded so you can ensure the overall stability of the containers and that they won't sway or move against wind loads or other weather conditions.

One thing you need to know about welding is that it cannot be easily undone or altered. Once you weld those containers together, and to the foundation, there is no changing that without great cost in terms of time, equipment, and manpower. Unlike some of the next approaches, welding is here to stay. So, remember that if you have any plans to move the container home or do changes to the overall structure; it will be nearly impossible if you've welded walls or floors to your foundation. This is the main challenge with this type of anchoring, though it provides the strongest and most stable connection between the containers or the foundation.

Bolting

It is possible to drill holes in the container's floors to bolt them to the foundation lying underneath it. The drilling is usually done around the 4 corners and then you can add 12 by 1 inches bolt. After that, you need to hammer those bolts into whichever foundation you have used, whether piers, piles, rafter, or trench. Finally, tighten the head of the bolt to ensure it won't shake loose.

As for connecting containers, you can also use bolting. It is not the cheapest option, but it guarantees stability and strength. You must bolt the containers together at adjacent corners for this to work. Drill through any corners in common between the containers, but add in a metal plate while you're drilling so it can act as a washer for the threaded sides of the bolts you will add later. Then, put in the bolts and add an additional washer on the bolt's threaded end and a nut to keep it from moving. Tighten the bolts and seal any gaps around both ends of the bolt using a sealant material.

Clamping

This is the cheapest option, but it is also the least durable and safe. Besides the fact that it is cheap, the plus side to clamping is that you can disassemble your containers and move them easily with this approach. It is not a permanent solution like welding, and it won't be as difficult to disassemble as bolting. In short, clamping is a great option if you plan on moving your container home in the future because you can easily disconnect the ties between the containers and move them to a different location.

Chapter 8.   Insulation

What is the key to turning an inhospitable metal box into a livable and comfortable 'real' home?

There's no doubt about it, it's insulation. Nothing can turn your exciting container home experience into an unbearable, sweltering, or freezing mess faster than skipping the vital step of insulating your container.

But for many, the wide array of insulation choices on offer can be confusing. This short guide will help you to understand the various types and assist you in choosing the one that's right for your climate, your needs, and your home.

Factors to consider: When figuring out what kind of insulation to use, several factors come into play including your budget, your particular environment, the effectiveness of each insulation method, and the long-term results they offer.

What Does Insulation Actually Achieve: Understanding R-Value

The purpose of insulation is to ensure that your home does not allow outdoor heat to enter it and remain trapped during warmer months and that it does not allow indoor heat to escape from it during cooler months. While no method of insulation can completely stop the process of heat transferal, a good method can certainly decrease it and this is indicated by an insulation method's R-value.

Therefore, a high R-value indicates an optimal insulation method that can markedly reduce the transfer of energy and a low R-value indicates a less effective method.

Now that we've established this let's take a close look at some of the most commonly preferred insulation methods being used by container home builders around the world:

Batting Insulation

Batting insulation is one of the most cost-effective and simple forms of insulating your container home. It generally consists of precut sections of fiberglass and can offer you a pretty good level of insulation in comparison to its low-price tag and ease of installation.

However, the major downfall of most batting insulation comes from improper installation. If you do choose this method, make sure that you focus on installing the batting correctly as one of the main causes of poor performance in batting insulation is the emergence of spaces or gaps in wrongly installed batting.

Note: Fiberglass bating should be handled with caution and installation requires the use of protective masks, gloves, glasses, and other protective gear.

Foam Insulation

Foam insulation is an excellent easy and quick method of insulation that really gets the job done. Although slightly pricier, my pick would definitely be spray foam. That's because it has the highest R-value and provides your home with real protection from the twin hazards of mold and container corrosion. No matter how awkward the space, spray foam insulation will easily fill it.

While industrial types of spray foam can provide you with incredible R-values, there's no reason why you can't manage to insulate very well with a normal hand-operated option. While there are 2 main types of spray foam namely open cell and closed cell spray foam, always make sure that you choose closed-cell polyurethane foam. This is because closed-cell foam is much denser and provides you with a much higher R-value than other types of foam. Closed-cell foam can give you an R-value of anywhere between 6.0 per inch all the way through to 7. 14 per inch, for stronger types, making it far superior to open-cell foams, which offer an R-value of only 3.5 per inch.

Aside from this resistance, closed-cell foam also gives you the added benefit of protection from degradation by water penetration. This is critical because any buildup of moisture can cause mold growth, making your home unhealthy.

In addition, closed-cell polyurethane spray foams are also great at keeping drafts out and ensuring that your container home maintains a stable, well-regulated temperature.

For these reasons, steer clear of open-cell spray foams that are far more permeable and provide drastically lower R-values, and reach for closed-cell spray foams instead.

Money-saving tip: Despite the slightly higher initial cost of closed-cell foam compared to open-cell foam, you'll be saving loads of money on expensive repairs and additional insulation measures in the future.

Another bonus of spray foam insulation as a whole is that it can be used on your container's internal and external walls, as well as on your container's underside, keeping damp and damaging mold at bay!

The foam sets quickly and can then act as a base onto which you can paint directly so decorating your container home is only a short step away.

Natural Insulation Methods

If you would like to keep your container home build as sustainable as possible, why not go for an eco-friendly insulation method?

People are now using a variety of materials ranging from cotton to wool and even straw bales to achieve all-natural insulation benefits. Let's take a look at some of the pros and cons of these methods.

Cotton and Wool Insulation

Cotton insulation basically refers to insulation blankets made out of cotton materials, usually recycled clothing. For this method, you will have to apply stud walls to place the blanket insulation into the spaces. It is applied in much the same way as fiberglass insulation and is as fast and easy to put up, but it does have a heftier price tag.

Wool insulation also replaces traditional fiberglass with pure sheep's wool and earns great environmental kudos because it can be created using much less energy than is needed to create fiberglass insulation.

Straw Bale Insulation

I know this may sound like a truly bizarre form of insulation, but it has provided container home builders with surprisingly consistent insulation benefits and is both cost-effective and all-natural.

First, plywood box beams are built alongside the container in order to support the bales of straw and provide a raised foundation. These beams also allow for space and airflow, ensuring that moisture buildup doesn't become a problem.

Second, a breathable type of plaster should be used on the straw bales, and no moisture barriers should be applied.

Third, the bales should be tied to the container in a few places with either galvanized wire or eyebolts.

That's it, a very simple method that gives great results. In fact, straw bales can provide R-value levels of up to R-30 or R-40!

A very important consideration to remember is that straw bale insulation only works well when your container home has a roof with big overhanging eaves. This is the best way to slope water far away from the walls.

Strawbale insulation has become a very popular method of insulating container homes, tiny homes, and other structures in recent years and with over 140 million tons of straw produced in the US alone and those living in rural areas able to access it for nearly free, it is also a very eco-friendly and extremely affordable way to regulate the temperature of your container home.

Money-saving tip: Don't bother hiring a professional builder for this method. If you have even the most basic building knowledge, a quick search online for 'How to insulate your container home with straw bales' will yield dozens of very detailed and easy-to-follow videos, allowing you to save on labor.

And for our final method of recommended insulation:

Insulation Panels

If you want to install your own insulation without help, insulation panels offer another awesome DIY option. Once you've got your stud walls up, it's very simple to purchase
panels in your needed size and from there, just place them into the spaces in your stud wall.

This ease of installation makes insulation panels one of the fastest methods using stud walls out there.

Even though panel insulation is comparable to the cost of fiberglass blanket insulation, it actually yields a very impressive R-value of about 7.5 per inch and is flat enough to save much-needed interior space, so your container won't be cramped.

Now that we've looked at the advantages and characteristics of these different methods, you'll be better equipped to make a final choice that works with your budget, schedule, and home.

Chapter 9. Services: Electricity, Plumbing, and Phone Line

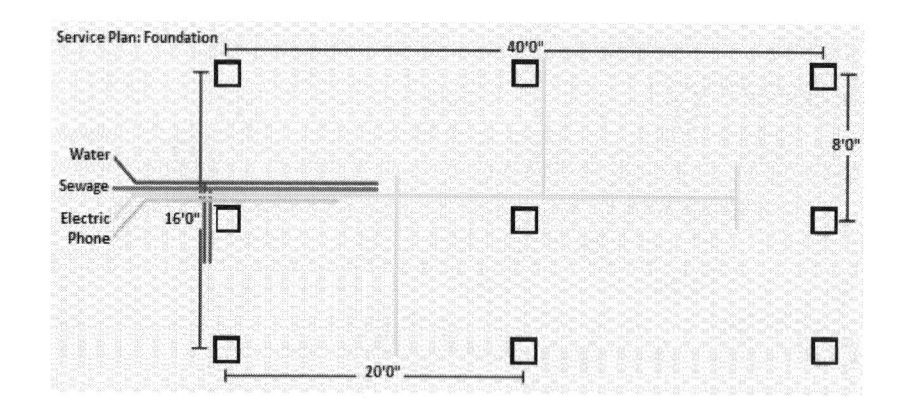

First Fix Services

The first fix services are one of the relatively early steps in preparing your site and your container. No home is complete without basic services. With first fix services, you run the electric, phone, and water onto the site. This also involves leading the water and sewage lines through the container. The telephone and electric lines can be run to boxes attached to the exterior, and then led through the wall of the container with a few simple drilled holes.

Just to get the terminology clear, the first fix services are all about making them accessible on-site. Drainage lines should be fit to run to the house drains to the city sewers, or, if you are building a bit away from the city, to a septic tank. The water main should be led from the city water supply or your on-site well to the water main for your structure. Make sure to install a valve to cut off the water main when you need to. Your electric and telephone lines can be run without having to attach the boxes to the container immediately, but it'll save you a few steps if you're able to make that happen.

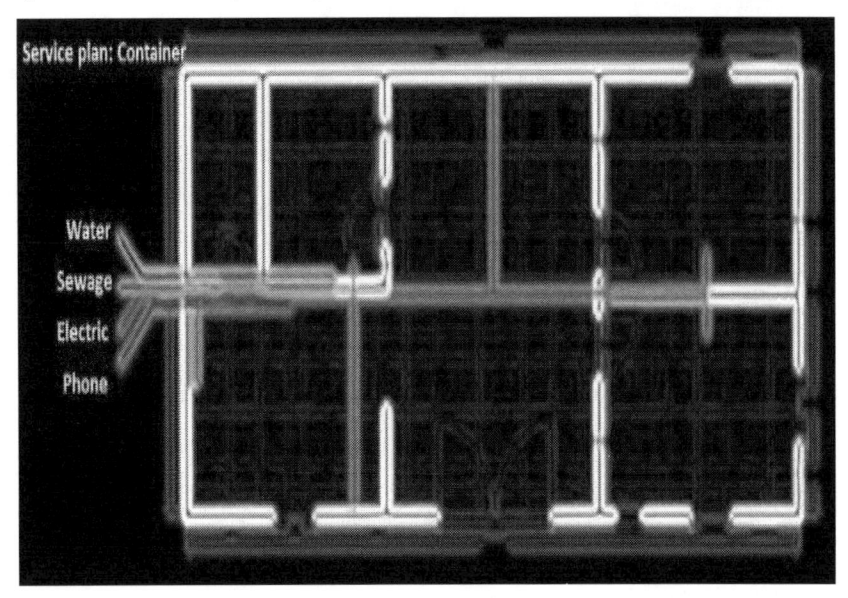

After you set up the first fix services, you're cleared to go ahead with flooring, framing the interior and the ceiling, and sorting out your insulation. After you've done all of this, you'll finally be ready for the second fix services. They will run your utilities from the outside of your container to all power sockets, lights, drains, faucets, and telephone jacks. It's a small project but it'll up the home factor of your new space exponentially.

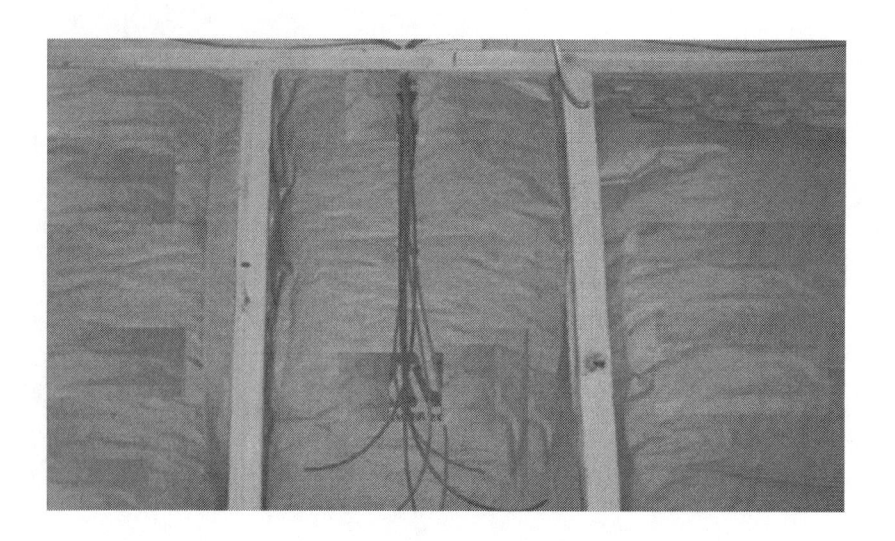

When making choices about your utilities, think about your foundation type. If you've opted for a trench or roof foundation, then you've already run your water and drainage pipes to where you'd like to place them inside the container. With piling or pier foundations, you won't have to think of the first fix until after placement. You'll have all the accessible space you need to drill some holes and lead the lines through.

When working with slab-on-grade or trench foundations, you can pre-cut the holes and then maneuver the container over the prepared line during placement. You won't have to worry about this for the electric or phone lines, as you can drill right through the container to lead those into the interior.

Remember, you should have a full plan of your finished home before taking the shovel to the ground. This means that proper planning can make sure that you factor in the water and sewage, situate the water main and drainage line relatively close together, and make it a simple process to run electric and phone lines throughout your home. It helps to have a plan page devoted entirely to services. This will make the marching orders clear when it comes time to install them.

Installing First Fix Services

We're getting into some of the technical bits with this part. You might need to hire an electrician to wire the box or a phone line technician to set up your telephone. And there's always the plumber. If you're a keen DIYer, you can definitely do that job, at least. However, if you can get a plumber on site to sort out the water main and main drain, that's one less headache. Or several fewer headaches, a whole bunch of Teflon tape, PVC, Joint compound, and other plumbing details that you just won't have to deal with. Once again, if your plans are well thought-out and clearly marked, that'll help to keep everyone on the same page and smooth out the construction process. This will save you some working hours and materials in the form of dead ends and costly mistakes.

Let's take a closer look at what's involved in the first fix:

Electric and Telephone Services

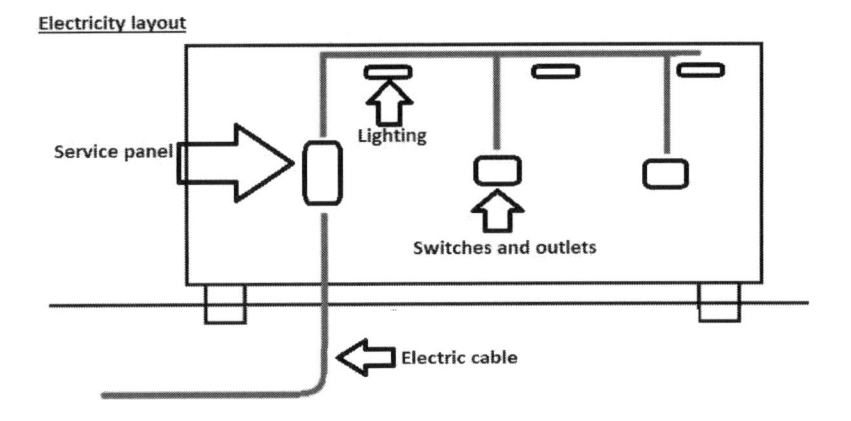

If you've been paying attention, you'll see right away that the image above depicts second and first fix services together. As far as electricity goes, the biggest question during the first fix is where you're going to place your service panel. You can either hang the line and run it under the roof of your container, or bury it and lead it up from the ground to the box. One thing to remember here is that welding the containers together will create the option of running the line between the boxes off the table. If this is the case, you're better off running the line underground. If you choose to weld the containers, then you will be unable to run the electric line between the containers. Running it underground and then leading it up into your container will be the only option.

Since we're talking about electricity here, it's worth it to mention that building regulations require them to be run by a certified technician. Plus, electricity can bite, so it helps to have someone with a proper background doing the deed. It's also important to remember that shipping containers are big metal boxes. Steel happens to conduct electricity quite well. So, grounding is essential. The whole structure should be earthed with a grounding rod to protect from electrical hazards. The line should be grounded as well. If you've got the know-how and can cover the building requirements, go ahead. Otherwise, see if you know someone or can hire a cheap contractor to make it happen.

You'll also notice that the telephone line isn't included in the diagram. It will require a different service box than the electric. However, if you plan it right, you can either use the same hole for both lines or place the 2 holes close together. The biggest deal at the moment is getting the line into the container. Now, if you'd like to set your site up with electrics before installing second fix services, you could always set up an outside electric box for your tools. This is a good option if you go for the DIY build.

Second fix electrics will require a framed interior. They take the electric line and run it to all of your lighting, switches, and plugs. An electric box is installed first. Next, the line is run from the electric box up through the ceiling and beside the studs of the walls. Once again, it's best to leave the proper installation to the technicians. Remember, though, that all the holes will need to be sealed well with mastic after the installation is over.

Installing Your Drains

Fitting water and sewage pipes

Your drains work on gravity. That means that all of the water that leaves the house travels down a pipe to go out of the home. You've got to maintain the downward slope of the destination for the length of the pipe. To bring your drain system into the container in the first place, you'll need to drill a hole. The pipe leading to the sewer or septic tank should be in place already. You can connect a vertical length of pipe to the drain and then seal around the hole.

As you're taking the water away from your home, you'll need to plan for a drop in elevation of a 1/4-inch per foot of length. This gives you a 1-inch drop for every 4 ft of the run. The idea is to steadily and gradually slope the water away from your home. If you absolutely need to reduce the drop, you can take it to the minimum of an 8 of 1 inch per foot of run. However, this will drop the length of travel that your system can take. So, if a 2 ft. drop from drain to sewage with a 1/4-in. the drop will comfortably take you 96 ft., you can expect 1 8-in. drop per foot to take you only 75 ft. After this point, friction can build up in the pipes to slow the rate of horizontal travel until you face blockages and backups.

Another key consideration is to look into the frost depths for the dead of winter in your area. You want to dig down and place the pipe below maximum frost depth. Your Geotech should be able to let you know how deep you have to go when placing the line. The last thing you need is an iced-closed drain during wintertime.

Finally, look into linking all your drains into one sewage runoff pipe. It's easier if you keep the bathrooms and kitchens as close as possible to the central drain. This is the way to go for the highest efficiency, but if you get fancy with the build, then you may need to extend the run-up a floor or to 2 drains placed on opposite ends of the structure.

Water Line Installation

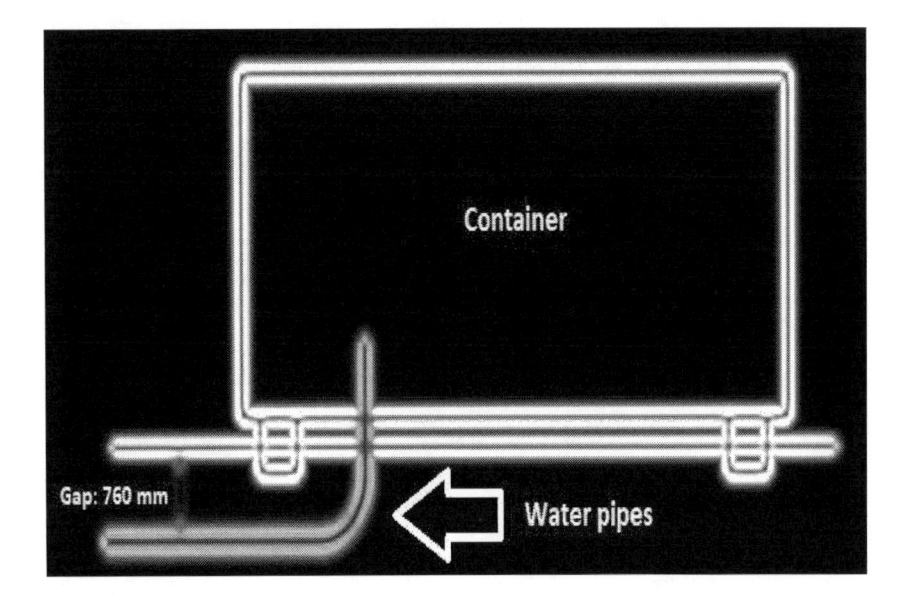

[Diagram showing container with water pipes below, labeled "Container", "Water pipes", and "Gap: 760 mm"]

The biggest difference between the water line and the sewage line is what drives them. Gravity versus pressure. Since the water main is pressure-driven, it doesn't matter if you lead the pipe upward to the destination.

When you want to run a water line to your structure, the first step is to dig a trench. If you're smart about this, you can set up the trench to house both water and sewage runs. There are also recommended inner widths for both sewage and water lines.

Here are some things to keep in mind:

- Dig down to at least 3.6 inches or 750 mm. to place your water pipe. This will make sure that you're below the frost depth for pretty much anywhere. Just check with the specifics from your local authority to be sure your build fits the code.

- Set the water line at least 14 inches, 350 mm, from any other services like electrics, sewage, or the phone line.
- One way to save time and space is to dig out a trench for all 4 and then backfill it with sand. This will make it easy for you to get to the lines when you need to while still protecting them from damage.
- Make the trench at least a foot (300 mm.) wide for a single pipe. If you're adding more, then expand the size of the trench.
- Use the same trench for the sewage and water lines, if not for all 4.
- Ignore the rise or fall for the water main, as it's pressure-driven.

Telephone Line Services

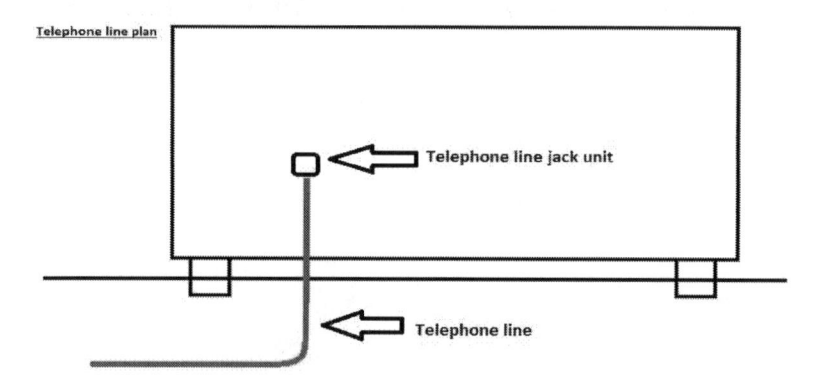

Just as the sewage and water lines can be run alongside one another, the phone line and electric line can be wired together. You can run the phone line directly through the container after drilling a hole. This is another feature it shares with the electric line. You can run it along with the electric line, lead it through the top, or lead the line through the bottom. So long as it reaches the telephone jack, you're good to go. If you go for the underground solution, raft and trench foundations will require you to set up the lines before pouring. You can run a length of PVC through the concrete and lead the lines later if you want. If you want to set out a path for the phone line, it can be run pretty easily through a PVC tube with an inner diameter of 22 mm. The biggest thing is to make sure that you can run the line from the exterior to the interior. Afterward, seal up any remaining holes or any excess room around your service lines with mastic.

Second Fix Services

The second fix service connects the utilities to all of the places that you will use them. Water lines are run from the main to all toilets and faucets. All the drains are installed in the home and led to the main drain. You will also have to run the phone line from the telephone jack and run the electricity from the main box to all lights, sockets, and plugs. Consider any other lines you'd like to run at this time as well. Doorbells, an antenna, it'll save time to install all of these things in a single go. Remember the order of operations when you're planning out this stage. You'll want to do it before you've finished the walls, and possibly the ceiling, depending on how you plan to run the lines. Some work with the drains and water line may need to be done before all of the floorings are finished. If you are building in the city, water is run to the city main and drainage to the city sewer. If your site is further out of the way, then you'll be working with a well and a septic tank.

Electric Services

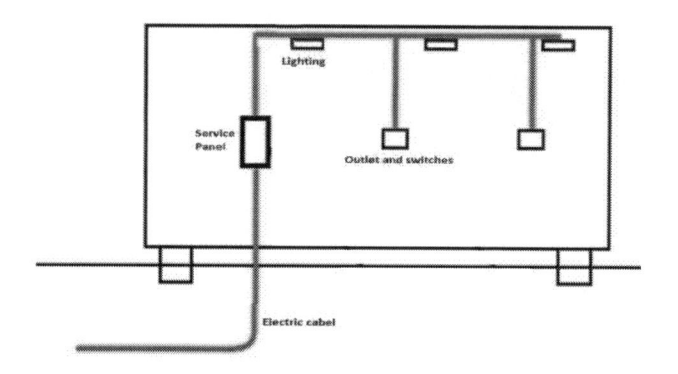

Depending on whether you install a ceiling before or after the electricity, you'll either be lining the ceiling or the roof of the container. If you plan to line the ceiling, you'll have to drill a hole through the ceiling to make space for the wires. This is the more aesthetic option. The wires will be hidden out of sight, leaving your container looking clean and uncluttered. The easiest way to do this is after placing the roof joists but before installing the ceiling panels. The other option is to run the lines along with the ceiling. This is a super simple solution. It will be visible after you run the line, but you can use a wire cover if you really like. If you're doing a DIY build, and want to make things as easy as possible, then this could be the way to go for you.

When dealing with the electrics, the goal is to run wires from the external electric box to all light sockets, light switches, and plugs. It helps to attach these to roof joists and wall studs, so you'll have to factor that in when placing wall and ceiling panels. It's also nice on the eyes to keep them all at a uniform level, but you can get creative here if you really want to. Try to go along the ceiling for the length of the container, and then branch down when you want to wire the bits you need.

A great solution for running your wire is Romex. This is a flexible, non-metallic cable that will hold up over the long run. You can also use trunking. This is plastic tubing designed to line and protect cables. You can then run the trunking where you need it to be. You can attach it to the joists and studs with tape wiring, plastic clips, or staples. However, if you don't want to work with trunking, you can run each wire individually and secure it with a tape wire.

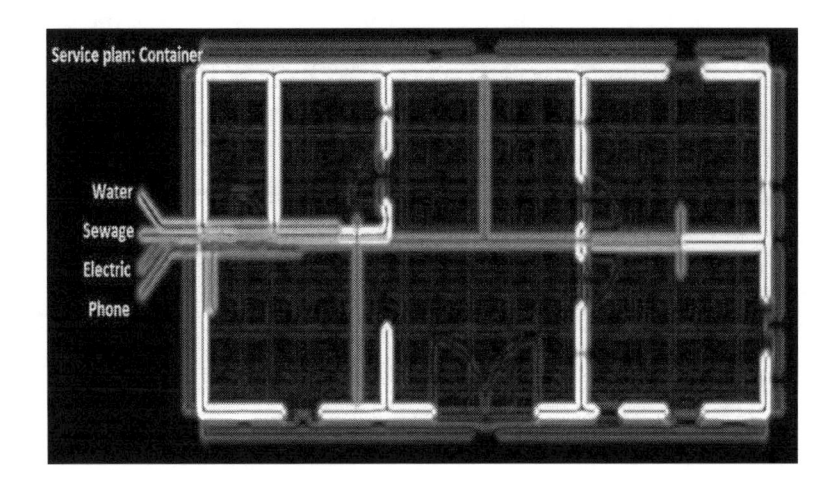

The diagram above offers an example for wiring the second-service electrics through the interior of your home. The blue lines give a possible path for running the electrics through the interior of your home to provide for outlets, light fixtures, and light switches. After placing the run of the electric lines, the next step is to attach the electric outlets, light fixtures, and light switches and to wire the electric lines into them. These should be affixed to the battens and roof joists to make them secure.

Remember: Electric work is dangerous and requires the skills and knowledge of an experienced technician. It's best to hire someone that knows what they're doing to avoid mishaps and make sure everything runs correctly.

Plumbing

![Sewage and water pipe]

When it comes to the second fix for water and sewage lines, you're talking about plumbing. This might be just a personal thing, but plumbing is a bit challenging. Setting up the line isn't the hard part; it's making sure that the joints are watertight and don't leak. You might be dealing with Teflon tape or pipe sealant, but the principle remains the same: make it tight enough to prevent leakage.

By this time, lines have been run for both the water main and the main drain. If for any reason, you don't have access to them from within the container, now is the time to make it happen. However, you should have vertical runs of pipe led up through the container so that you can lead them to the drains, showers, toilets, and faucets. Just remember that everywhere you're running water, you're also running drainage. You'll save a lot of time by doing both runs at once. If you've planned ahead, you'll also have some floor space removed to handle the plumbing beneath. It probably goes without mention that this step should be done before finishing the flooring.

The pipes must now be prepared for all sinks, showers, and toilets. Run the plumbing so that all drains lead to the sewage drain, and all water pipes to the water main. Also, install stop valves so you can shut off the water when you need.

Water and sewage are pretty straightforward regarding second-fix services. Just run all the drains to the main sewage output and run all the faucets, toilets, and showers to the water main. This is where the clever designs are helpful. If you've done it right, you'll be using an absolute minimum of pipe and working hours to provide water services to your home.

Chapter 10. Renewable Energies

Solar Panels: Hot Water and Electricity

Solar panels are important for your shipping container home. They provide hot water and electricity, and they're relatively inexpensive to install.

For instance, a solar water heating system will cost around $2000 initially and about $500 annually after the initial installation. A solar electric system will cost about $3000 initially and about $800 annually after installation.

However, the financial benefits of adding either or both of these systems to your shipping container home can be worth it in the long run because you'll save money on energy bills while reducing your carbon footprint!

If you're currently using hot water from the tap, you'll really benefit from having a solar water heating system installed. The amount of money that you'll be able to save each year depends on several factors, including the amount of hot water your family uses, the number of people in your household, your current energy provider's price per unit, and whether or not you have any other energy sources besides electricity.

The average solar water heating system will provide 90% of the hot water consumed by a family of four and it'll save you roughly $450 per year on energy bills.

To calculate how much money, you'll actually save each year, multiply your family's hot water usage by $.08 for electricity and $.27 for natural gas (which is generally the cost of just one unit of natural gas).

For instance, if your family uses 30 gallons of hot water each week then you'll be saving about $39 every month on energy bills alone!

Be sure to take into consideration any additional costs that might pop up due to having this system installed, such as installation costs or maintenance fees.

If you'd like to learn how much money you can save on electricity each year with a solar energy system, simply do the same calculations that you did for the hot water system and then multiply it by $.16 (the average cost of one unit of electricity).

For instance, if your family uses 15 units of electricity each week then you'll be saving about $60 every month on energy bills alone!

Make sure to consider any additional fees for having a solar energy system installed.

Regardless of whether or not you decide to have a solar water heating system installed, it's still important to have a backup source of hot water available.

How Much Solar Power Do I Need?

Solar panels can be used to supply almost all of the electricity required for a home. However, it's important to have a backup source of electricity in case your solar panels aren't producing enough electricity or if they fail during a summer storm or power outage.

To determine how much extra electricity that you'll need, multiply the average amount of usage by two. For instance, if your household uses an average of 15 units of electricity each week then you'll need to have a backup source of 30 units.

That way you'll have enough to get by until the sun comes back out again or until the system is fixed!

If you're interested in installing a solar panel system, consider buying it outright instead of leasing it. Leasing a solar panel system can end up costing twice as much over time, and that doesn't seem very cost-effective when you think about how much money that that could save!

Installing Solar Panels

If you decide to install a solar panel system, make sure to read the manual for your solar panels because it contains a lot of useful information about how to maintain and operate the system. Installation is relatively easy, but you'll need to have someone experienced with electrical work lend a hand.

If you're planning on having a professional install your system then be sure that they're licensed and registered in your state. You should also ask lots of questions about the process beforehand so that you know what to expect.

You can save money by purchasing materials for these systems yourself and doing much of the installation yourself. You can find instructions on how to build small solar panel systems online or you can contact a solar energy company to have an installer do the work for you!

To summarize, if you're interested in installing a solar panel system, be sure that they're installed by an experienced professional who's licensed and registered in your state. You should also ask lots of questions about the process beforehand so that you know what to expect.

Assemble Your System Before You Install It

Even though most solar panels come already assembled, it's still nice to make sure that everything is perfectly level before you put it together. That way everything will be even all around and it'll be easier to keep everything aligned during the installation process.

You can do this by driving a few stakes into the ground to help anchor the panels in place later. You can also use a string or drill a hole through each panel, lace the string through it, and then pull the panels in one after another until they're perfectly level. It'll take several passes for this all to be done, but it's much easier than if you were installing them one panel at a time.

It's also important to note that asphalt roofs are not ideal for the installation of solar panels. If you're already on an asphalt roof then consider removing some of the top layers to allow more sunlight through, but be sure to have a plan for this before you remove any layers!

The initial installation process can be a little bit complicated, but once you have everything set up it should be easy going from there. That being said, it's still a good idea to have someone who knows what they're doing check your solar panel system periodically to make sure that everything's working as expected

Chapter 11. Flooring

Replacing the Plywood Floors

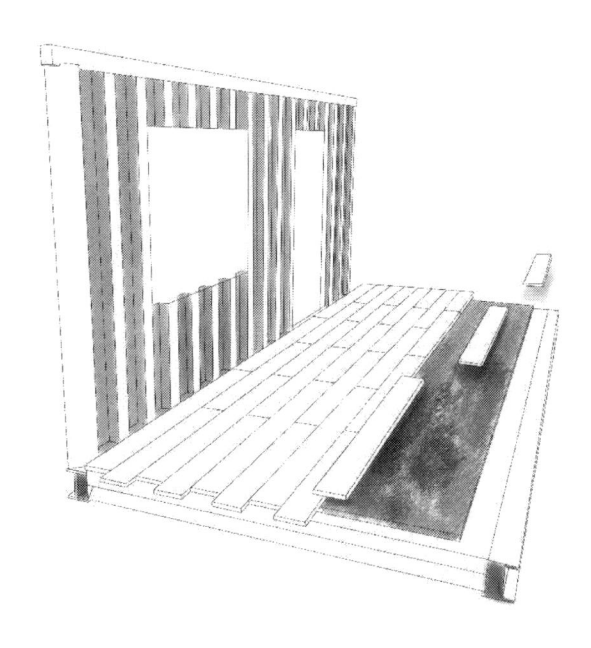

Do you have to remove the plywood floors and replace them? No, you don't. Is it a good idea? Yes, it definitely is. Different factors play into this decision, starting with your budget, but most people remove the original shipping container plywood floors and replace them with new floors just to be on the safe side. It certainly is the safest option, and you won't have to worry about the kind of chemicals that might be lingering on the wooden floors. So, assuming you want to go forward with this, how can you remove the existing plywood floors?

- **Removing floor bolts:** You need to start by cutting the floor bolts first. You can use a handsaw or a reciprocating saw, whichever you have in your toolbox. Locate the floor bolts first; you will find them at 12 inch spacing along with the cross members. Do this step delicately to avoid damaging the container's underside and, more important, wear protective goggles.
- **Removing the floor:** Next, get a pry bar and remove the floor panels by forcing them up and then toss them out of the container. There isn't much to this task, but it could take a lot of time, especially if you're dealing with a 40 ft. container rather than a 20 ft. one. After removing the existing floors, you can add in the new ones.
- **Insulate:** The great thing about getting rid of the plywood floors is that it makes it a lot easier to apply insulation to that part of the container. Normally, isolating the container's underside is tricky, and it has to be done when a crane is lifting the containers. But when you remove the floor, you have access to the floor's cross members, so you could apply spray foam or panel insulation here before adding in the new floors.

Then you can install any kind of floor you want. The underside of the container is insulated, the chemically laced plywood floors are removed, and all that is left is for you to add to the new floor.

Keeping the Plywood Floor

As we mentioned earlier, you don't necessarily have to remove the plywood floors if you don't want to do it, but there are some things that you should do to minimize the risks. Here's what you can do.

Remember that you can add waterproofing sheets before adding subfloors or anything else to ensure that your floors' permeability is minimal, as shown in the below diagram.

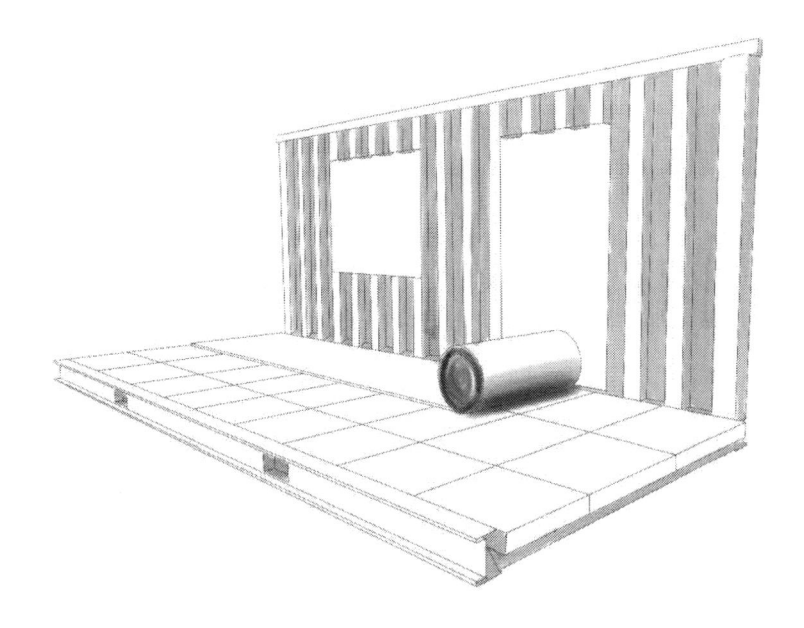

Install Subfloors

If the existing plywood floors aren't seriously damaged, and you want to keep them, you can add a subfloor. This will help you avoid the hazard of any possible chemicals that might be lingering in the plywood seeping into your living space. To ensure that those chemicals on the floor are contained, you first need to seal the floor. Start with cleaning the existing plywood thoroughly, you can use isopropyl alcohol for that task. Then, add a coat of low viscosity epoxy, which has an excellent ability to contain moisture and works perfectly in damp conditions. One epoxy coat is usually enough to seal the floor, but you can use two to be extra sure.

Leave the epoxy to dry so it can contain any harmful vapors that might be leaking from the original floor. It would be good to add a layer of foam insulation to provide even more insulation to the entire house. Then install a layer of marine plywood over the layers of foam and epoxy. After that, drill through the new and original plywood layers with screws to fix the new floor.

Treating the Original Floors

If adding a subfloor isn't something you are interested in, and you'd just like to keep the original floor as is, then you will need to treat it first. As we mentioned earlier, the risk with the original plywood floors of the containers lies in the fact that they might emit hazardous vapors and fumes, whether from earlier added pesticides or shipments. To get rid of those fumes, you need to contain them. For that purpose, we will also use epoxy here. It is the perfect sealant for this case, and it will stop any fumes from seeping into the rest of the house. You'll also want to clean the floor with alcohol before adding the epoxy.

Concrete

This is another option you have if you want to keep the original flooring. The great thing about concrete is that you will not need to add epoxy to seal in the floor or add a subfloor. You will just pour the concrete directly on the original plywood floor, and it will create a natural sealant layer when it dries. The concrete can also be the finished product, so this will be the floor you will use around your shipping container home.

A lot of perks come with using concrete for the floors. It is easy to clean, it is quite durable, and can last for quite a few years. You can also work with concrete and make the design yours. It can be dyed if you want to change the color or polish it and give it a shiny finish. The downside of using concrete is it absorbs cold, so it might be colder during wintertime. Another downside to using concrete is that it requires steel enforcement as we mentioned earlier, though this step is not as complicated as you might think. You'll just add steel bars across the length and width of your floors to form a grid, but make sure they are at least 1 inch higher than the original plywood. Weld them at a distance of one foot from one another and pour your concrete.

Finishing Touches

Adding in new floors or leaving the original one (after treating it) isn't the end of flooring renovations. Get the work done on the container's flooring before you get to work on dressing the interior and framing. After that, it is time to add some finishing touches to the floors. Concrete aside, you can add in tiles, carpeting, or a new laminate layer to cover your floors. Many people choose hardwood floors but those cost more.

One thing you need to consider while figuring out how you want to finish your floors is the weather. In a warmer climate, you don't want a floor that can radiate heat, but rather one that can help you cool down. A great option here is concrete as we mentioned earlier, but you can also use tiles and laminate too. These floors store cold temperatures and help keep your living space cool when the weather is hot. On the other hand, if you live in a colder area, carpet is your best choice because it doesn't transfer cold as much as concrete or tiles. The downside to carpeting is that it is a bit more exhausting to clean, but it gives you warmth in cold weather which makes up for that problem.

Adding Tiles

The great thing about tiles is that they are easy to clean and they can come in amazing designs you will love, and they keep the house cool in hot weather. When you place the tiles, the safest bet is placing them along the shipping container's width and length, whose dimensions help make this a lot simpler and you won't need too many special cuts. While you can add in the tiles before or after framing the interior, it's suggested that you add them afterward. Putting the tiles before framing the walls means you must cut the tiles to fit the steel corrugation, but if you do it after framing, you will just cut the tiles as you would with any traditional home.

Placing the tiles might sound easy, but it is a bit trickier than you might think; there is an art to it. You have to know where to start and which pattern you would like to follow because there are quite a few options. You can tile the place from one wall and make your way to the opposite wall, placing them row by row. Or you can start at the center of the container and move from there, which is ideal if you want to set the tiles diagonally or in a certain pattern; still, this approach means you will cut all the tiles that are adjacent to the walls. If you plan to make a pattern or alternating colors, you need to try it out first by arranging your tiles before you start the process. See a mockup of how it would look and what might work and what might not work.

This will also help you work quickly since the adhesive sets pretty fast, so you need to know what you're doing and what tiles go next. In short, prepare before you start setting the tiles in a certain pattern, it will save you a lot of time and effort. Some people do tile for a living, so it might not be as easy as you think, which is why you should keep to a simple pattern if you have never worked with tile.

For the adhesive, you have a few options. You could use either thin-set mortar (a mixture of cement, water, and fine sand) or tile adhesive for floors. The mortar sets in about a full day, and you shouldn't walk or place anything on it until the full 24 hours expire. On the other hand, floor tile adhesive sets much quicker, depending on the type you are using. It is also a lot easier to work with, especially if you are new to all this. The problem with adhesive is that its water-resistance capabilities are not good. It can easily mold if you have high water inflow from a flood, for instance, and will lose its adhesive power. The adhesive also might suffer if there's constant, significant movement on it for extended durations. Thin-set mortar is more durable and has higher water resistance abilities. It's best to use adhesive with vinyl and linoleum, while the mortar is best used with ceramic tiles and porcelain.

Be careful while using both mortar and adhesive because they dry up pretty fast, so don't cover large spaces while working. Instead, take it one small space at a time and then place the tiles in the area where the adhesive is. Lay the material and cover as much space as you can work in ten minutes or so. Put the first tile, press on it, and move on to the next one. Always use tile spacers on the corners because they help you keep proper alignment between the tiles and you will avoid small changes in the angles, which can be problematic in the future. Make sure the tiles are properly leveled; you can use a spirit level for that. Work all the tiles using the same approach.

While it would save you a lot of time directly placing the tiles over the plywood of a subfloor, the tiling might not come out evenly. Some experts recommend adding a layer of concrete over the plywood floor to make sure the surface is smooth and even, and then you can add your tiles, which will ensure a much more even finish. Concrete is also a much better surface to use with mortar or floor adhesive.

Carpeting

If you're living in a colder climate, then carpeting is definitely the best choice, especially if you like to walk around your home barefoot. You can also add in the carpet if you like how it looks and feels, and the great thing about carpeting is that it gives you a lot of options in terms of design and aesthetics. The main challenge you will face with carpeting is that it is more cumbersome to clean, but on the plus side, it is easy to place.

You can't just lay the carpet on your shipping container floors, though. You need to first add carpet grippers, thin pieces of wood with pointy pins protruding from one side, to hold the carpet's edges in place. So, add the carpet grippers at the edges of the container or the room you want to be lined with carpet, and make sure the grippers are either nailed to the floor or safely in place using adhesive. Make sure you leave a small space of 1 cm between the grippers and the walls. Next, the smart thing is to add carpet underlay, which will provide comfortable cushioning and make the carpets a lot easier to walk on. A standard carpet underlay has foam on one side and rubber on the other, and you need to place that latter part down on the grippers and unroll it from wall to wall. Remove any excess underlay by cutting it with a blade. Do the same with any area with carpets and make sure the underlay is comfortably placed on the carpet grippers. Connect any gaps between overlay layers using carpet tape to avoid having any level inconsistencies in your carpet.

Then you can place the carpet you have chosen. Cut the exact dimensions that make the carpet fit comfortably in the room, and do the same with other rooms in the house. While placing the carpet, start at a corner, and make sure it is secured into the carpet gripper. Leave a space of around 2 inches since the carpet will stretch. Once you're done with the first corner, move to the next one along the wall, attaching the carpet to the grippers along the way and fitting it properly. Have a utility knife on you so you can cut off any excess carpet and help it fit perfectly in the room.

Laminate Floors

Laminate flooring is one of the best and most elegant solutions for finishing the floors, but it is best done after framing the house's interior. It is easy to add and you can put it over a subfloor or an overlay, so that certainly makes things simpler. The best way to start with laminate tiles is to start at the far end of the room, placing the tiles from left to right, and working your way until you reach the opposite side—the door. Do the same for each room, but adjust accordingly. It is always best to work from the side opposite the door and work your way until you reach the threshold.

Laminate flooring often comes with tongue and grooves so you can fit each tile into the next one. Slide the one you have in your hand at an inclined angle against the one already placed, lower it, and then comfortably slide it against the tile until it is securely in place. Do the same with all tiles until you finish the first row and do the same moving forward. You might need to cut the last tile in a row so it can fit the space, and you have to get the measurements right with this. Put the new tile over the old one, mark the length you need for it to fit, and cut along your marking and then place it.

Remember that it is always advisable to leave laminate floors until you are done with framing the interior walls, or else you must cut the laminate tiles to fit the corrugation of the steel wall as we mentioned earlier. So, it's always best to frame the walls first so you won't have to spend so much time on this consuming process. Another tip, while working with laminate, would be smart and alternate the joints; you can do that by using any discarded sections from the preceding row and starting with it on the next one. This is important because it ensures that joints would never line up against one another.

Chapter 12. Rooftop

Roofing and installation choices are just as important as any other aspect of preparing your shipping container home prior to moving in. Choices may be limited depending on geographic location.

As always recommended, check with your local building department to make sure that your choice is not only legal, but appropriate for your city, county, or state ordinances.

In some places, you may decide to simply go with the metal top of your shipping container, especially if your container placement is only temporary. However, do be aware that leaving the steel roof unprotected from the environment can accelerate corrosion and/or possible damage depending on climate scenarios.

Roofing your shipping container home comes with a number of pros and cons.

Pros

- Protects the roof from inclement weather
- Aids in insulating against cold or heat
- Protects the steel container from puddling water and helps to protect against rust and corrosion

Cons

- More cost outlay
- The necessity to adhere to local building codes

If you've decided to go with a roof, your next step will be to decide which type!

Roof Types

Suitable roof types are suitable for shipping container homes:

- Flat roof
- Sloped roof (often called a shed roof)
- Raised or gable roof (will require trusses—not typical but an option)
- "Green" roof—traditional with pioneers and early American settlers, sod or earthen roofs are also an option

Carefully consider each option depending on aesthetics, cost, and local building regulations.

Individuals looking to move into a shipping container home are often ecological-minded. For those, a green roof or earthen roof provides a number of benefits.

They enhance installation capabilities, reducing heating and cooling costs. They're natural and aesthetically pleasing, relatively low maintenance, and they're fun!

Before deciding on a green/earthen roof, however, be aware that you'll need to waterproof the ceiling of the shipping container with a membrane or other roofing material to protect the structure against damage.

Tip: Remember that your shipping container also needs to be strong enough to support a sod roof! Consult with a building or roofing expert to determine the load limitations of your steel container depending on size.

Every type of roof construction must also follow local building regulations in regard to slope or pitch.

Preparing for a "Green" Roof

Several steps are necessary before you simply cut out chunks of grass and place them on top of your shipping container. First, verify slope specifications with your local building department.

You'll need to follow a few steps before you "plant" your green roof:

- Some type of waterproof membrane will offer protection to the top surface of the shipping container.
- Sheeting that will act as a root barrier. Polyethylene is one choice.
- Some type of aggregate (pebbles or mesh for example) to enhance drainage when it rains.
- Some type of filtering fabric such as burlap or weed barrier paper. This is common in landscaping scenarios to prevent weed growth. Weed barrier paper or fabric blocks the sun, preventing the growth of weeds. Be aware of the difference between landscaping fabric and filtering fabric. Both are geotextiles but landscaping fabric serves as a barrier while draining fabric serves as a filter.
- Planting soil/fertilizer/nutrient-rich dirt that will provide nutritional support for sod.

- Grass, low-growing and shallow root groundcover, or other choices.

Flat Roofing

Flat roof shingles or asphalt shingle rolls are an option for covering the top flat surface of the shipping container. Application methods will depend on the type of materials chosen.

Tip: A flat roof is not conducive to a number of geographic locations around the US such as those that receive heavy snowfall in the winter months.

Sloped or Shed/Angled Roofing

Sloped or shed roofing is recommended in areas that receive a lot of snow in the winter. They're also conducive to the installation of solar panels. Pitch requirements may be quite specific depending on your geographical location.

Regardless of the pitch or slope of the roof, choose materials that will not only provide the insulation factor and protection you'll need depending on the environment, but that will not only match the ultimate plans for the exterior of your home with local ordinances and preferences.

For example:

- Asphalt shingles (wood shingles are rarely used in the US anymore due to potential fire dangers).
- Asphalt shingle role (tarpaper, adhesive, and easy roll-out application make for easy, fast installation).
- Galvanized or metal roofing (coated steel) is preferable in areas that get a lot of snow.

Points to remember:

- No matter what type of roof you choose, opt for one that is structurally sound, suited for your environment, and that your shipping container (based on size), can easily bear.
- Green roofs are beautiful, ecological, and low maintenance, but they are also extremely heavy. Be aware that additional steel support columns may be required inside the shipping container to evenly distribute the weight.

Tip: Before designing or deciding on a roof, refer to the expertise of a structural engineer to will expertly provide calculations for support as well as load limitations of your shipping container.

Chapter 13. Interiors

This part of the project is when your hands get dirty, and you will need all the tools you can get, from plasma torches to cutting wheels. It would be a good idea to consult with a structural engineer at this point as well to ask about which walls can be removed and what you should avoid preserving the structural integrity of the shipping container.

So, where should you start with converting the container?

Adjoining Containers

One of the most common changes that people make while converting shipping container homes is opening up adjoining containers to increase the floor space or make more room. Many people think that working with metal is hard or impossible, but not if you have the right tools and you know what to do. Either way, you must cut through a lot of walls to make room for doors and windows and open up your containers. Cutting through metal might seem daunting, but it is actually easy because, if you do it right, the results can be outstanding and clean. It is a material that can be shaped however you like, which is helpful.

Removing the walls between two adjoining containers only seems logical to increase the living space and make it one big container, considering the tight space inside a single shipping container. The first thing you need to do is mark and measure the walls you need to remove if dealing with multiple containers. It is also a good idea to consider what you want to do with the doors before working on the walls. Let's say you have 3 containers next to each other. For example, will you leave all 3 doors intact? Or maybe you want to incorporate them into the design somehow. Your last option would be welding them shut and treating them as an ordinary wall.

Installation of an Auxiliary Container Joining Structure

The trick to working on adjoining containers properly is to set them next to each other exactly as you want them to be. If the conversion was done off-site, this would be the only concern you have and the one thing you have to do right. But if you are converting on-site, it is a whole other story. Remember to make sure that the containers are well connected to each other with bolts, welds, or clamps before you get to work on the adjoining walls. Then, go to work using a cutting wheel or a plasma torch and remove the wall's space you want to remove. This might be the entire wall or just a part of it, depending on your design, which is why you need to measure and mark the parts you want to cut before getting to work.

It would be smart to line the container's adjoining faces with spray foam if you won't be cutting the whole wall, allowing the remaining parts of the wall to have insulation. After cutting the walls, weld steel plates in the gaps between both openings to secure the container walls' structural integrity, but not after spraying the insulation if you hadn't already done it. Then, simply connect the pieces together and finish.

If the conversion was done off-site, you would just have to make sure the openings are aligned, and the interior walls are also aligned properly. Having clear plans from the get-go will help you with this part since you will know exactly where the removed walls will be and how to align the containers accurately. Whether you are converting on-site or off-site, double check your measurements and markings because this is one area where incorrect measurements can be problematic. Also, double-check the steel plate connections between adjoining walls and roofs and make sure there are no loose parts here or there since those can jeopardize the entire house's structural integrity.

Pro tip: Wear protective gear, including gloves, goggles, and/or face shields if possible. Cut metal is sharp and can be dangerous, and you will have your hand around it often in this phase, so you should take safety precautions.

Floors

Some people forget to weld the floors after they're done with cutting through the walls. Just as you welded the remainder of the walls with steel plates, you need to do the same with the floors to turn the multiple containers into just one unit—the last thing you need is to walk into your house after it is done to find gaps between the floors. Aesthetics aside, welding the floors together also strengthens your shipping container home's structural integrity and naturally eliminates the chances of any pests sneaking in from the floors or leaks happening.

One last very important detail here is the structural reinforcement if you plan on removing large chunks of the adjoining walls. In that case, you need to use steel box beams to support the load coming from the roof and ceiling, and they need to run across the width of the containers in which you have made those large cuts. Stitch-weld the steel beams to the interior of the container roof. As always, consult with a structural engineer here to tell you exactly the bearing loads that need to be supported by the beams so you can understand which kind to get and of what dimensions.

The great thing about dealing with adjoining walls is that you have a lot of options here. Many container homeowners like to create archways between the two adjoining containers, which increases the space and looks elegant, and gives the illusion that the floor space is bigger than it is. If archways aren't your thing, you can separate the wall between adjoining containers into segments, with some leading to rooms and others leading to a shared living space, for instance. The possibilities are endless, and making changes through adjoining walls is easy enough to give you that flexibility.

Doors and Windows

With the walls now open between the containers, your shipping container home should be taking shape quite nicely. Next, you need to start working on the doors and windows and the frames you need for each. The first step to working on windows and doors is taking their measurements and marking their locations on the walls. As always, these measurements need to be accurate, and they have to be double-checked because you will be changing the frame of the container, so you can't afford to make any mistakes here. Some experts recommend using cardboard templates for all the doors and windows you will be working on and marking those. Get it right the first time.

Then, cut through the container walls following the measurements you've taken for the doors and windows. Use plasma torches, cutting wheels, and whatever tools you find necessary to do the job. Also, as with converting the walls, remember to wear protective gear because those cut parts will be sharp and can injure you if you are not careful. Ensure all rough edges are smoothed and fill any gaps in the metal walls with a sealant to ensure that your shipping container home is watertight and won't allow pests in. Next is creating the frames for the doors and windows, and after that, you install the doors and windows and hang them to the frames.

Making the Openings

To make the openings for walls and frames, the process is pretty much the same as cutting through the container walls to make more space. Like before, take accurate measurements of the required opening and mark it on the container wall. As we mentioned earlier, you can use a cardboard model of the window (don't forget to include the frame), which will help you get exact measurements. Then, cut through the walls with a torch or other tools.

A plasma cutter is probably the best tool to use here because it gives the cleanest lines and the steel you cut can be reused, unlike other tools that might damage that spare steel. If you can't get your hands on one or don't know how to use it, you can make do with an angle grinder that will do the job, though managing that tool is complicated because it doesn't easily make straight lines, so you must be patient. Last but not least, use a flap disk to smooth the edges and the opening.

How to Make the Frames

Before installing the doors and windows, you need to make the frames, making your container pop and look like a real home. You can either order prefab frames designed for doors and windows, or you can make them. You could make a square out of galvanized steel tubes with 50 x 50 mm. dimensions and cut several lengths of them for the frame. After that, put the frames against the doors and windows to ensure that the measurements are correct. If they fit, remove the doors and windows and stitch-weld the frame. For aesthetics and extra protection, smooth the constructed frame, and then spray-paint it with galvanized paint to resist corrosion.

Now, you have your openings and your frames to weld the frames to the container after cleaning the edges and making sure they are smooth. After that, it is time to hang the doors and windows.

How to Install Doors and Windows

After welding the frames to the opening, you have already made, installing the doors and windows is time. Next, hang your walls and windows into the fixed frames and weld them together. You can also use self-tapping screws here to secure the windows and doors in place if you are not handy with welding, though welding is a more durable option and requires less maintenance in the long run. Remember to fill any gaps between the frames and the container with a sealant to maintain its structural integrity—pay special attention to the corners because they are the weakest part of the frame. You should repaint any metal parts with galvanized paint because they might become exposed during the installation process.

Chapter 14. Exterior

Finishing the exterior of your container, like every step of the process, offers a number of options. One of the key considerations in this process is whether or not you have insulated the exterior of your container. Though you will be able to finish the exterior of the container with cladding even if you have placed foam insulation on the exterior, it will be far more challenging and will compromise your insulation. Therefore, here are some recommended methods for finishing the exterior of your home, depending upon the insulation of the exterior.

Finishing an Exterior with External Insulation

If you have placed spray foam insulation on the exterior of your home, then you have only a few recommended options. The first is to paint, and the next is to cover the insulation with stucco. Either way, you will want to ensure that your insulation is covered and sealed. When closed-cell polyurethane is exposed to sunlight, it begins to degrade. Paint or stucco will ensure that your insulation remains intact and retains its integrity.

Painting Exterior Insulation

When painting over exterior insulation, remember to use either latex paint or water-based acrylic. Oil-based paints can damage the foam of the insulation. Avoid high-gloss paints, as these will highlight any unevenness in the underlying surface. Flat or semi-gloss paints will help to cover the insulation and provide an aesthetic finish.

Prior to painting, walk around the container and keep an eye out for rough edges. If you do see any rough edges, sand them down with sandpaper. Remember to wear a facemask in the process to avoid inhaling particles of insulation.

Once all rough edges have been removed, you can cover the exterior with paint. Use a minimum of 3 coats. It can be applied with either a spray gun, roller, or thick brush. Spray guns are the quickest option and offer the most consistent paint cover. Make sure to gauge the paint flow on scrap cardboard before beginning application. Rollers will be slightly slower but will get the job done effectively. Paintbrushes offer the best control but get the slowest results.

Tips: You may choose to apply a wax sealant to cover the paint once it has been applied. You will get a better finish if you use several thin coats rather than a single or few thick coats. Each layer should be allowed to dry before applying a new one.

Rendering or Stuccoing the Exterior

If you choose to stucco the exterior of your home, it is best to first ensure that the spray foam insulation has been applied with a rough finish. This will ensure that the surface has more texture for the stucco to grip. Since the render is just for the finish, there's no need to go overboard with it. You can simply purchase just-add-water mixes. Each 20 kg bag will offer 5 mm of cover to a 2.5 m^2 (50 ft^2) of surface area.

The first step in applying stucco to your home is to fix beading to the corners with adhesive, ensuring that the beading is straight. Cover the ground around the exterior of your home with thick plastic sheets. Mix the stucco powder in a bucket with water, and allow it to stand for 5 minutes. While waiting, wet the external insulation down with a hose, providing a damp surface for the stucco to affix to.

Begin applying the stucco from the bottom of the container and work upwards, using a steel trowel. Use long strokes to ensure that it is applied evenly across the surface. Make sure that all stucco is applied within 30 minutes after mixing. As with paint, it is better to place the stucco in multiple thin layers rather than a few thick ones. Try to keep each layer about 5 mm. Rake each layer after application and while still wet. This will offer grip for the next layer. Finish the last layer with a polystyrene float, giving a nice finish to the stucco.

Finishing an Exterior without External Insulation

If you have chosen to leave the exterior of your container home bare of insulation, then you can finish it in a number of ways. One of the simplest, easiest, and cheapest is to leave it bare. This showcases the origin of your home and can be quite aesthetically pleasing, as well as a tangible indication of what you have accomplished in the creation of your home.

If you choose not to leave it bare, then you can either paint the surface or clad it with wood. Leaving the containers plain offers no more explanation, so the following will explore the process of both painting and cladding with wood.

Painting Your Container

While leaving your container bare can leave a legacy as to the origins of your container, it also leaves it susceptible to the elements. By adding a layer of paint, you protect against rust and increase the longevity of your homes.

The first step is to prepare your containers. Peel off any stickers and clean the surface of your containers. You can use a razor blade if the stickers are proving difficult to remove by hand. Should any rust remain, remove it with sandpaper, grinders, or wire brushes. You will also want to cover the ground surrounding your container with thick plastic sheets.

The best paint to apply to the exterior is alkyd enamel paint. This can be applied to the exterior either with brushes, rollers, or spray guns. As described above, spray guns are the fastest option and provide the most consistent cover. Rollers are slightly slower, but can still offer a fairly consistent cover. Paintbrushes offer the most control but require the most skill to ensure a consistent application. Use a minimum of 3 coats when applying exterior paint.

Timber Cladding Your Exterior

The final option that we will explore in this manual for finishing the exterior of your home is cladding it with timber. This offers an aesthetically pleasing option, giving your home the external appearance of wood home. It is light and quick to fit, and it can also provide an additional layer of protection to the exterior of your home.

The first step in timber cladding your home is to fit the battens: 2 x 4 inches planks are ideal for this process, and it is best to fit them to the size of the container before framing your container. Fit the battens 400 mm. (16 inches) apart. Fix them to the container by drilling a hole through the end of each batten 1 ft. from both floor and roof. Drive a bolt through this hole and tighten a bolt on the inside of the container to hold the batten in place.

After the battens have been affixed at the top and bottom, drill a hole in each foot and repeat the process, tightening a screw on the inside of the container for each one. The battens will be attached to the container securely.

Once your battens are in place around the perimeter of the container, you will be able to attach cladding to them. Cladding is essentially wooden boards nailed onto the exterior battens. The process is essentially the same as adding real wood to the interior walls. Nail the cladding into the battens using stainless steel nails. Begin at the bottom of the battens and work your way up to the top. Overlap the joints of the cladding as shown in the figure below. Once the cladding has been placed, treat it with a moisture and UV resistant coating.

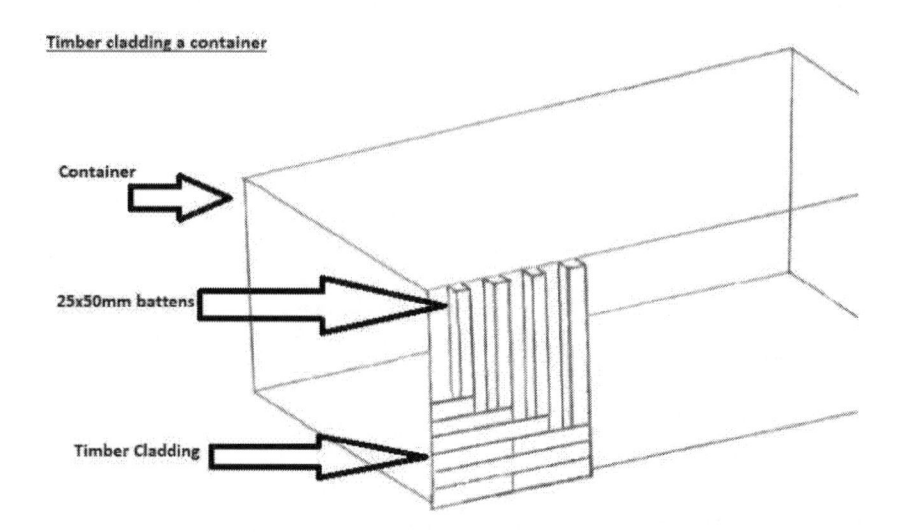

Chapter 15. Tips in Choosing a Container

Choosing a container to use as a home or office isn't as easy as some people would think. Perhaps the easiest part is to go down to the shipyard where all the containers are stacked up and paying for it. That's basically it.

Most of the information you glean off the internet or from books is the choosing part. Why do most people leave out this very important detail? Well, basically because it is a very boring, tedious, and time-consuming task that doesn't pique anyone's interest at all.

But, if you're planning on getting a container to turn it into a home or an office, you need to deal with this very specific detail. You need to pay attention to everything concerning the container before you even reach into your pocket to pay for it.

So, let's start with some of the key things you need to look out for: The Price and the condition or state that the container is in when you see it. These two can fluctuate greatly based on your assessment and negotiation with the shipyard manager.

Subsequently, the worse the shape the container is in, the lower the price you can get it for. Some people may scoff at this as the general mentality towards buying anything is to get the highest quality at the best price. This can be a little bit more flexible for containers especially if your plans fit the current condition, it's in for the price you can agree on.

If, for example, you're going to cut out huge chunks of the container, there's little to no sense of buying one that's in pristine condition. Although it basically means that there's going to be little to no repair work done to it after cutting huge portions of your container—that's not just cost-effective as you're led to think.

Moving on, let's talk about the price:

Price of Containers

The going price for a container in pristine condition also depends on the size of the container. This also depends highly on the location of the shipyard and its distance from the construction site. These are things you have to pay attention to as they can really affect the price of the container. As for the basic price of the container, a 40-footer can cost you anywhere from around $1400 to 1600. Everything else after that, like transportation and the rental of a crane, is entirely up to you.

Size of the Container

When you start planning to create a container home or office, you're going to encounter the consideration of size. For example, you can't have a 40-footer in a small lot nor would it be practical to have a very small container to serve as a full-time home. Simply put, the size of your container is very crucial to your plans and the realization of the project.

Type of the Container

By now everybody already knows what a container basically looks like. What not everyone knows is that there are actually a lot of different types of containers. For example: what everyone already knows about containers is that there is a 20 ft. and 40 ft. variety. But then there's an even bigger, as well as smaller, container that is also available for people to use in their designs. There are 45 footers and 10 footers out there that you could incorporate into your design.

Here are the types of containers and what you could possibly do with them:

- **Standard containers:** These are the containers you regularly see as container structures like container homes or offices.
- **Hi-cube containers:** These are fantastic as the high ceiling space adds more roominess to the entire structure. These are also the second most popular type of containers (regardless of size) made into container structures.
- **Open-top containers:** Open-top containers have tarpaulins instead of metal roofs to cover them. These can be used just like a standard container but instead of having the metal roof you can devise one out of any material you so choose. This is perfect for those who are planning to have high roofs not necessarily made of metal.
- **Open containers:** These containers basically just comprise 4 solid posts. These can be used as connecting rooms to other containers and can either be boarded up to remove the exposed areas or left as is to have an open-air space in between 2 or more containers without deviating from the basic plan of having a container structure.

Condition of the Container

Containers are essentially complete by themselves and can be used immediately as a home or office with little to no modifications done to it. Now, based on your plan, you have to look at the condition of the container to ascertain if this is the one you need for your container structure. Ideally, one in pristine condition is the container to go for but if you're going to cut large portions out of it, you might as well look for containers that have some damage in the parts you intend to cut off.

For example: If you're going to cut out a huge section of the sidewall to connect it with another container, just look for a container that has major damage in that area. Not only is this a very cost-efficient way to go (damaged containers sell for less than that with little to no damage at all) but it will also make your work faster as the damaged sections are already compromised and can easily be removed with minimal effort.

Assess your plan and buy accordingly.

Chapter 16. Organization and Design Hacks for Your Container Home

A standard shipping container home can provide enough space but one in limited quantities. In this case, it would be best for the homeowner to adapt to a minimalist lifestyle or improve on their organizational skills around the house. Aside from choosing to apply multiple functionalities per area of the house, simple practices of organizing things around the home can do a lot of good. Here are some organizational and design hacks that will be well worth the knowledge. Not only will they allow for a cleaner-looking space but over time, they will help homeowners focus more on what they need instead of what they simply want.

Bedroom

The bedroom is one of the most if not the most important part of any home as it offers a place for rest, relaxation, and refuge. This is why it should be kept organized at all times. Although clutter does foster creativity, it keeps the mind awake and alert. At a time when a person only wants nothing but to rest, this is not the best thing in the world, for the brain to remain active when it should not be. Especially in a standard shipping container home where space allotment is quite limited, using the right furnishings and keeping personal belongings intact is highly necessary.

Adapting to a minimalist lifestyle may be a challenge at first but it can be extremely rewarding later on. The thing about minimalism is not restricting ownership but focusing on the important things, what is essential around the house, what has a function; needs versus wants. Not only will it help you with the organization but it will also help you save money for other, more necessary, purposes.

In the bedroom, the essential pieces of furniture include the bed, a closet, and a bedside table. These days, there are plenty of available sources for multi-functional furniture. This can mean having storage underneath the bed frame, a nightstand that can function as transformable seating, and a closet that can have a built-in dresser.

To further maximize the space and keep the bedroom serene, be selective when it comes to the choice of color. Go with light pastels or calming earth tones like tans and greys. Accent it with white or cream molding for an elegant overall look. Keep the window treatments as simple as you can but never ignore function. These should be thick enough to keep most of the light out but not too thick that they make the space look smaller than it actually is.

Everything that is not supposed to be part of the bedroom should be kept elsewhere. If there is a room in the shipping container house that needs the most effort, it is this. Make sure that it is a place for rest and nothing else.

Living Area

The living area will surely be the busiest part of the house. It will also be the primary area where homeowners will be entertaining visitors and guests over time. This is the reason why, even with a limited amount of space, ample seating may be required. It is a good thing that there are plenty of furniture offerings these days that allow for multiple functionalities.

A compact living room set up in a traditional single unit intermodal shipping container home.

The living area is where the entertainment section should be. For a typical modern-day homeowner, this may include a television set and its accompanying sound system and video playback equipment. Depending on the homeowner type, video game consoles might also be a part of the equation. Flat-screen television sets are all the rage these days and in a shipping container home, these are ideal because they carry a sleek design and can easily be hung from the wall.

Again, by taking advantage of and maximizing the available vertical space, you can keep things off the floors and maximize the visible horizontal area in your shipping container home. If the wall structure permits, all wiring can be drawn through the walls into a common exit point lessening the look of clutter from multiple cords.

Then comes seating. A comfortable sofa is important. Since the area will be the busiest one in the home, there should be no question when it comes to the need to invest in good furniture. If you are the type of homeowner who frequently has guests over, it will be a good idea to purchase a convertible sofa bed. It can work well as seating during the day but also allow you to provide a cozy bed for people staying overnight. The best part is that the bed can conveniently be tucked back into place after usage. No muss, no fuss.

Additional seating and storage can be provided by box ottomans. These can also double as end tables for the living room. Simply position a piece of glass or wood atop it and you have yourself a makeshift coffee table centerpiece. When it comes to lighting fixtures, again, suspended varieties work best.

Kitchen

In a shipping container home, it is important for sufficient ventilation to be applied to the kitchen area especially if homeowners are active cooks. With the help of a structural engineer, several windows can be cut from the steel cargo unit and replaced with efficient exhaust systems. This is a very important initial step that should never be ignored.

When the ventilation has been taken care of, homeowners should then address the function of the kitchen. Will it be used solely for cooking and food preparation or will it double as a breakfast nook if not a dining area as well? If the space will only be used as a designated kitchen for cooking, then homeowners should invest in the appliances that they need.

Most home kitchens come equipped with a stovetop, an oven, an overhead exhaust, a microwave, a toaster, and a coffee maker. Sounds like much but these are the basic appliances that go into a typical kitchen. If the allotted space and budget allow for all of these to be purchased then by all means purchase them. If the homeowner wants to keep the space simple but still have that food prep function then the toaster, coffee maker, and microwave may be scrapped from the list. It is fairly easy to heat meals, boil water for coffee, and toast bread on the stovetop.

Here is an industrial-inspired kitchen in a shipping container home. Notice that it has all of the important components that a kitchen needs yet is arranged in such a way that gives the perspective of a wide and open space. (Image from www.containerhome.info)

The necessity of the stovetop and oven is self-explanatory. As for the overhead exhaust, in addition to the kitchen windows and general exhaust system, it will easily help homeowners control food smells that can penetrate walls and furniture. It also works tremendously well in controlling the excess heat that may circulate around the kitchen and the shipping container home. As it is positioned directly above the stovetop, it can immediately absorb the emitted heat and food smells while the homeowner cooks.

If the kitchen will double as a dining area, sufficient dining and seating provisions should be considered. This means that homeowners should invest in a table for starters. If there is a limited amount of space to work with, a kitchen island can work well as a preparation area and dining table in the kitchen. A makeshift bar can also be considered in this case. It can easily double as a room partition and the homeowner can take advantage of its multi-functionality. The number of chairs depends on how many people live in the home. Usually, 4 seats are the standard. If there is enough space to work with, this can be extended to eight followed by a round table that can be used to entertain guests. If the available space is limited, 2–4 chairs will work just fine. Provided that there is multi-function furniture in other areas of the house, like the living room perhaps, these can then be used for extra seating when needed.

In a shipping container home, a pantry can be built into the structure much like a bedroom closet. When homeowners go for the built-in storage, they can easily maximize the vertical space allotment in their homes. Further, increase the amount of available storage by having retractable shelving installed in the main pantry cabinet. These will make for more storage that can be accessed with ease. Just a quick pull will give homeowners access to the ingredients that they need for the meal they are preparing.

Just like the other parts of the home, be sure to have a place for everything. A drawer for cutlery, cupboards for plates and the like, storage walls for pots and pans, and so on and so forth. An organized kitchen will not only allow for a cleaner space but one that is easy to work in as well.

Bathroom

A shipping container home can provide ample space for a bathroom. Utilizing the streamlined approach will make it appear bigger than it actually is. Here is an example of a bathroom used in a single container home.

Now comes the bathroom. The rule of thumbs for bathrooms is that they should be kept as simple as possible but able to satisfy all of the homeowners' needs. There are only 4 components necessary to make a bathroom complete. Here they are:

- Sink
- Toilet
- Shower area
- Storage for towels and toiletries

For most people, the sink is the first thing they use when they enter the bathroom upon waking up. They wash their face, brush and floss their teeth, and proceed with their daily regimen from there. There is really no need to spend a lot of money on a sink because it provides a fairly basic function. The important component that homeowners should pay attention to is the faucet. This fixture is important as it controls the amount of water being pumped onto the sink. A long-headed curved faucet works best by offering a substantial amount of space between the water source and the sink. This extra space makes it easier for homeowners to wash their faces, collect water, and the like. It allows for less water wastage too. For the knobs, go with traditional spin knobs instead of the variety that runs on sensors.

The toilet. Unlike the sink, it will be a wise decision to spend a bit more on the toilet fixture. These need to be durable enough to handle the daily wear and tear and should be large enough to offer a comfortable experience to those using them. Aside from the size and quality of the toilet, homeowners should also invest money in the flushing system. These days, there are multiple mode systems that help conserve water. These come with 2-3 buttons. Each button is designated to release a certain amount of water when pressed so homeowners do not have to resort to a full flush, one that empties the entire water reservoir, every single time.

And then comes the shower. Homeowners that have ample space and a higher working budget can equip their shipping container home with a bathtub and shower setup. Those who only have the option of choosing one of these normally go for the traditional shower. This part of the bathroom is pretty simple to address. All that is needed is enough space for a person to move in. It would be best to apply tiles to the designated area from the floor to about half of the wall. This allows for easy maintenance. The tile also protects the outer wall from excess water exposure. To control water flow, have a half-foot barrier built on the floor separating the shower area from the rest of the bathroom. Use either a shower curtain or a glass partition to complete the look.

Finally, a complementary feature to any bathroom at home is the storage cabinet for towels and toiletries. A common practice is having a shelf or 2 installed underneath the sink again utilizing the available vertical space to save on the horizontal one. If there is ample ceiling space, homeowners can also choose to have a cabinet built from the ceiling down to about a third of the total wall. The cabinet is meant for towels, paper napkins, toiletries, and all other products needed for a bathroom and nothing else.

Conclusion

Thank you for making it through to the end of this book. These rusty old things we call shipping containers have quite a few benefits for an unsuspecting and needy world. There have been several grassroots projects to use shipping containers as alternative housing in poverty-stricken countries and they have also been used as temporary shelters for victims of natural disasters. There are a plethora of ways that the standard shipping container can be used to make the world a better place. Here are a few of the best examples:

Shipping Container Housing for the Poor

Container homes are a great way to provide affordable housing for the less fortunate. Shipping container homes have been placed in economically deprived areas all over the world in order to put a roof over the financially poorer among us. All you have to do is have a crane to put one down throw on some insulation, install basic electricity and plumbing and you have yourself a great low-income housing unit. The trend is now catching on worldwide and even in the poorest of regions; whether in the economically deprived American South or South Africa these sturdy shipping containers of yore are providing a great place to live for those who really need it.

Shipping Container Dorms for Students

College students are usually a little bit strapped for cash with all of their tuition expenses and the price of books. This usually relegates them to overcrowded college dormitories they can't afford or to living in a rundown house in a rough, crime-infested part of town with 10 other roommates to split the bill! But in many parts of the world universities have jumped on the bandwagon of the shipping container and have created whole student apartment complexes.

Simply by stacking several containers on top of each other they have produced instant student housing! Some of these professionally designed student apartments have rent as low as $ 200 a month! This is unheard of at most other college campuses. Some even come complete with high-speed internet! Get ready to benefit university students; because these sleek shipping container dorms are the wave of the future!

Shipping Container Hurricane Relief Shelters

With the insane number of hurricanes that much of North America has been subjected to in recent times, hurricane relief shelters have been a much-needed resource. After the U.S. was pummeled by brutal storms such as Harvey, Irma, and Maria in rapid succession emergency relief organizations such as FEMA were running out of places to put the survivors. It was out of this necessity that many had the idea of simply dropping shipping containers off in affected regions such as Texas, Florida, and Puerto Rico. These shelters are ready-made, and with the most minor of modifications, they can be made into a perfect relief shelter for those who need it so desperately.

Shipping Container Military Barracks

The military has actually been using shipping containers as temporary barracks for a while now. Predating the commercial sector's use of shipping containers as homes by several decades, they were even used during the first Iraq War in 1991. These freighters can happily withstand a barrage of weapons fire so dropping these guys down on an enemy beachhead for troops to seek shelter in is of great advantage.

Shipping Containers to Scale Back Your Footprint

Everybody talks about their environmental footprint nowadays and how they can reduce it. But a shipping container is a means of reducing your impact on this planet almost entirely! You can live in one of these metal hulks and not put any extra strain on the ecosystem whatsoever. You are not using any harmful materials in it its construction and if you opt for solar, you don't even have to plug into the grid! Another reason that shipping conditions are so good for the planet is the fact that you are basically recycling sturdy building material that would otherwise have ended up in a landfill. So yes, use these shipping containers to scale back that footprint of yours!

As strange as it may sound, shipping containers could very well be life-changing in their scope. The idea that you can use something such as a shipping container, which has been sent all over the world to ports far and wide can be used for permanent housing is nothing short of remarkable. These freighters are built perfectly for the job and with a very minimal amount of effort and finances just about anyone can be a proud new shipping container homeowner! Keep your eyes peeled folks, and keep looking to the horizon because your ship has arrived!

Made in United States
Orlando, FL
27 March 2024